PREHIST
SETTLEMENTS

PREHISTORIC SETTLEMENTS

Robert Bewley

TEMPUS

Dedicated to Jill, Hannah, Fiona and Richard

First published 2003

PUBLISHED IN THE UNITED KINGDOM BY:
Tempus Publishing Ltd
The Mill, Brimscombe Port
Stroud, Gloucestershire GL5 2QG

PUBLISHED IN THE UNITED STATES OF AMERICA BY:
Tempus Publishing Inc.
2 Cumberland Street
Charleston, SC 29401

British Library Cataloguing in Publication Data.
A catalogue record for this book is available from the British Library.

ISBN 0 7524 2547 1

Typesetting and origination by Tempus Publishing.
Printed in Great Britain by Midway Colour Print, Wiltshire.

CONTENTS

ACKNOWLEDGEMENTS

Without the initial request to write this book from Stephen Johnson and the continual support of my wife, Jill, this book would not have been possible. The help of archaeologists in Britain and Ireland has been a great bonus, many have willingly offered information, advice and illustrations. I am grateful to Martyn Barber, David Buckley, Tim Champion, Mark Corney, Peter Crew, Andrew Fleming, Paula Gardiner, Frank Green, J.D. Hill, Terry James, George Lambrick, David Miles, Diana Murray, Chris Musson, Adrian Olivier, Rog Palmer, Mike Parker Pearson, Francis Pryor, Peter Reynolds, Peter Rowley-Conwy, Colin Richards, Blaise Vyner, Humphrey Welfare and Helen Winton for their help, discussions and comments. Particular thanks are due to John and Bryony Coles for all their help and encouragement and the information about Glastonbury Lake Village. I am also very grateful to Stephen Johnson and Peter Kemmis Betty for their comments on earlier drafts of the text.

The following institutions and individuals provided information, photographs and illustrations: Mr R. Besley, Bill Britnell of Clwyd-Powys Archaelogical Trust, Cambridge University Collection of Air Photographs (now the Unit for Landscape Modelling), Cleveland Archaeology Section, John and Bryony Coles, Chris Cox, Simon Crutchley, Debora Cunliffe, Andrew David, Ken Davies, Peter and Lysbeth Drewett, Derek Edwards, Essex County Archaeology Section, Andrew Fleming, Damian Grady, Helen Glass (Rail Link Engineering), Frank Green, Vince Griffin, Jim Hancock, Dennis Harding, Alan Hardy, Peter Horne, Terry James, Terry Manby, David Miles, Chris Musson, the Ordnance Survey, Oxford Archaeology, Andy Payne (in supplying the illustrations of the geophysical surveys of hillforts), Dominic Powlesland, Derek Simpson, Ian Ralston, Peter Reynolds, Ben Robinson, Royal Commission on the Historical Monuments of England, Royal Commission on the Ancient and Historical Monuments of Scotland, Phil Sinton, John Vallender and Geoffrey Wainwright. A special debt of gratitude is owed to Sarah Prince and other English Heritage staff; in the NMR, Lindsay Jones and Katy Whitaker (and for the first edition especially Clare King, formerly of RCHME), and in Scotland the RCAHMS staff for assisting with the provision of so many aerial photographs and plans. The work of Judith Dobie (English Heritage) and David Williams on the illustrations deserves special praise and thanks.

I am also grateful to Tim Clarke and Michelle Burns for their efficiency during the production of this edition.

PREFACE

A book which covers such a broad topic as prehistoric settlements cannot cover all the subject and needs to be selective. This book is no exception. It is not intended to be a catalogue of settlements in Britain; that would be a task worth doing but is not the purpose here. The picture presented is in some ways a reflection of my own discovery of archaeology which has centred on survey and settlements, but it is also a reflection of current thinking about archaeology and the constant need to interpret and re-interpret the past. Archaeology is not a static subject and new information, through survey and excavation, means that we have to constantly update our thinking and approaches. Sometimes these new discoveries are accidental and immediately force us to change our perceptions; at other times the revelations are as a result of archaeological projects which have taken a decade or more to provide us with a new approach.

The book also concentrates on England, which is more a reflection of my own knowledge and not in any way meant to reduce the importance of Scotland, Wales and Ireland, whose prehistoric archaeology is amongst the best in western Europe. Further reading for these countries is listed at the end. The Palaeolithic period has been left out completely, not through any lack of interest but because it requires a complete book to itself.

Many archaeologists are moving away from the Three-Age system of stone, bronze and iron, because these technological changes are not equivalent to all the changes in the archaeological record. They are, however, convenient divisions for separating the settlement evidence but they should not be seen as watersheds in prehistory. The gradual changes which took place throughout the prehistoric period are evident from the settlements, burials, ritual and industrial sites.

Preface to Tempus edition (2003)

It had always been my intention to revise this book but to re-name it Prehistoric Landscapes; yet when Peter Kemmis Betty asked me to update it for Tempus, I realised that there had been an enormous amount of information generated on prehistoric settlements in the decade 1993-2003. Knowing the book is used by 'A' level and undergraduate students, I thought it might be useful to characterise some of the results and new ideas which have emerged since 1993.

In summary, there has been a dramatic increase in the discovery of sites of all types and periods through survey, but excavations have revealed a number of neolithic houses – Yarnton in Oxfordshire and White Horse Stone in Kent spring to mind immediately but there have been a number of discoveries elsewhere. The increase in the use of geophysical surveys has also made a significant contribution to what we already know about individual sites (for example, hillforts) as well as in landscape studies, especially in the Danebury environs project. The impact of 'television archaeology' has also been very significant in the discoveries it has made; not just *Time Team* but a whole variety of others, including *Meet the Ancestors*. The result of the programmes has been to greatly increase the interest of archaeology with the general public, but also to provide the opportunity for research, which aims to answer a very simple question – 'what is it?' An example is the discovery of a Bronze Age wooden installation of the foreshore of the River Thames in London, investigated by the *Time Team* crew: a clear manifestation that the Thames was as important in prehistory as it is today.

There has also been a transformation in archaeological thought over the past decade in our understanding of the forces of change. In my formative years as an archaeologist the words 'diffusion' and 'migration' were seen to be traditional and 'old-hat'; the so-called new archaeology and its descendants were (rightly) looking for a deeper meaning in the material cultural remains of the past. These two dynamic forces of change, migration especially, were nearly unwitting casualties. However, they are beginning to be re-evaluated in prehistory (and in Anglo-Saxon studies), partly because of events in the last decade; we are the products of our times and the ending of the Cold War and the problems in the Middle East opened up a movement of peoples across and beyond Europe. Refugees, asylum seekers and other people on the move are visible again. Thus, the diffusionist theories of the pre-war era, based on concepts of the movement of peoples, invasion and migration are now worthy of discussion and debate; ideas do not just move from one society to another without human interaction.

Interpretations based on historical (or archaeological) research are open to abuse in that we may wish to impose a past which highlights the positive aspects of human behaviour where 'peaceful migrations allowed for one culture to supersede another'; the evidence, however, so often points to a cruel and bloody past. We know from our everyday experience that people who come into contact and are seen as 'foreign' to each other, invariably engage in some form of conflict. The evidence at a remove of two or more thousand years can be difficult to detect but it is there, often as absence of evidence. The settlements and landscapes were abandoned and changed, sometimes through natural disasters but more often than not through conflict, as is so well illustrated from the finds at Crickley Hill.

Finally, the increase in discoveries through survey, and especially aerial survey, has been dramatic. In part this has been through the luck of some dry summers in the early and mid 1990s (see the section on Iron Age sites and banjos in southern England). But it has also been through the interpretation, mapping and recording of archaeological sites visible on aerial photographs that the most discoveries are being made. English Heritage's National Mapping Programme is referred to often and there are a few highlighted samples of these new discoveries.

1

INTRODUCTION

the past must be **I**nvented
the future **M**ust be
rev**I** sed
doing bo**T**h
m **A**kes
wha**T**
the present **I**s
disc**O** very
Never stops

A mesostic by John Cage

As a guide to prehistoric settlements this introductory chapter shows the way in which archaeology has thrown light on 'prehistory' and how we have arrived at the present definition of 'settlements'. There is a plentiful supply of traditional guides to prehistoric archaeological sites and these are listed under further reading. The purpose of this book is to answer four basic questions:

1. Where are the prehistoric settlements of Britain?
2. What form do these settlements take?
3. How old are these sites and landscapes?
4. How do archaeologists study settlements?

The first three questions are the most frequently asked of any prehistorian and therefore it is justifiable to present this book as an answer to some of these questions. The fourth question will be answered as a theme running through the book. Examples of the way in which archaeologists use their data and manipulate the results – the act of which is not without contention – appear in every chapter. Some of these will be familiar; for example, radiocarbon dating is now a widely understood technique. Other techniques such as dendrochronology or spatial analysis using Thiessen polygons may be less familiar.

There are no absolute answers in archaeology and especially in prehistory. Archaeology as a discipline can provide a framework on which to hang various interpretations. The study of prehistory is a comparatively new subject; the term prehistory was first used as a title to a book, *Pre-historic Times* by John Lubbock (later Lord Avebury) in 1865. The hyphen between the 'pre' and 'history' is important as the term conflicted with religious (western) beliefs in challenging the antiquity of the Earth and Man's place within it. Lubbock was asking questions which we today are still trying to answer; some of the more straightforward ones about date are being answered but the questions of social structure and political organisation are subject to the same prejudices and fashions which Lubbock had to fight against in 1865. The intellectual atmosphere when he was writing was very different from today; Darwin's *Origin of Species* was still four years away from being published, in 1869. Lubbock was bringing concepts about the antiquity of Man to a readership thoroughly imbued with the date of creation as 4004 BC: 'The first appearance of man in Europe dates back to a period so remote, that neither history, nor even tradition, can throw light on his origin, or mode of life.' Others at the time (Palgrave in this case), whom Lubbock quotes say, 'We must give it up, that speechless past; whether fact or chronology, doctrine or mythology; whether in Europe, Asia, Africa or America; at Thebes or Palenque, a Lycian shore or Salisbury Plain; lost is lost; gone is gone for ever' (**1**).

This book is about that 'speechless past' and how for the last 140 years people have not given up studying it but have been trying to find out more about it. Although beyond the scope of this book, it is interesting to contemplate why as a species, *homo sapiens*, we are so interested in our past; we seem to have an innate desire, even a need, to know from whence we came.

1 *Knook Camp, Salisbury Plain, Wiltshire. Salisbury Plain has areas of chalk grassland in England which have not been ploughed for over 2000 years, and the survival of earthworks is therefore very good.* Cambridge University Collection of Air Photographs: copyright reserved

Prehistory took over 50 years to become accepted in the wider popular terminology; a local society was formed in 1908 called the Prehistoric Society for East Anglia and in 1935 this became the internationally renowned Prehistoric Society. This Society is now an international organisation with over 2,000 individual members from professors and practising archaeologists to those who form the bulk of the membership, the interested amateur (see further reading for more information about the Society and its publications). Despite the obvious interest in prehistory the revised education system in England, introduced in 1991, does not allow the teaching of prehistoric archaeology as a core subject. The arrival of the Romans is the starting point for teaching British history; it is hoped that readers of this book will be able to use it to redress this classical imbalance.

Archaeology and prehistory have their own imbalances; it can be argued that the majority of prehistory, at least until the Iron Age, is based on the study of the dead. This is mainly due to the very good survival of the monuments that were erected for the dead: long barrows, round barrows, dolmen, chambered tombs and passage graves. The study of settlements is a much more recent research topic but no less interesting for that. However, the distinction between the living and the dead, settlement and ritual, is a modern construction. We have to be aware that what we might interpret as a particular category of site might have performed several functions which involved the everyday 'domestic' functions as well as the 'ritual' functions or vice versa. The sites known as 'causewayed enclosures' are included here, not because we know that they were settlements or were ritual sites, but because they are important (non-burial) sites within the society of the time and are, therefore, part of the landscape which included settlements. They have been included because we do not, in all honesty, know what they are (**26-9** and **colour plate 11**). Defining their use might prove as difficult as defining the use of a parish hall if there were not the records to show the many uses of a hall, most of which have nothing to do with ritual (Christian) activities in the strictest sense of that term.

Another imbalance concerns the material which prehistorians have at their disposal. There are no written records to give an insight into the ideas and activities of these communities; there are only the material remains of past societies, that have not completely decayed, and it is only a proportion of these material remains which are recovered by the archaeologist. This is a fundamental point to stress; the prehistorian does not know what the total recoverable amount of material there is or was. Therefore, what material we have to deal with is a sample of a sample, the total size of which can never be known. Added to this are the raw data, the bones, stones, organic material (leather, wood, and environmental information), which survive in different locations at different rates; in technical jargon the 'post-depositional factors' coupled with 'site formation processes' (the study of how the material left at a site was deposited) are very important to the prehistorian. With every interpretation, be it functionally, environmentally or socially determined, the first question is whether the pattern which has been revealed is as a result of deliberate human activity or as a result of more than 2,000 years of decay and disruption.

This can apply as much to individual sites as it can to landscapes, and it would have been possible to alter the title of this book to include the word 'landscape'; prehistoric people had their own cognitive geography. Our landscape is different and we have imposed our own semi-scientific ideas on them in an attempt to understand their formation, geologically and archaeologically. If we take the evidence from the Somerset Levels or the Fens of East Anglia, to gain some understanding of prehistoric life, we are able to show what life in prehistoric times was like in those areas, but it does not give us the total picture for Britain. We cannot extrapolate from the low-lying peat of the Levels to the highlands of Dartmoor or Bodmin Moor, or the chalk lands of southern and eastern England, or further afield to Scotland or France, even though the settlements may be contemporary.

Fox's *Personality of Britain*, published in 1932, influenced a generation of archaeologists and affected the way they conceived the British Isles. He proposed a distinction between a Highland Zone and a Lowland Zone as a good starting point for understanding early settlement (**2**). Apart from extensive use of distribution maps, which are fundamental to so many archaeological studies, Fox's Zones were meant to reflect cultural differences. His approach is seen now as too environmentally deterministic, despite its influence on many archaeologists. In 1972 Chris Taylor, echoing Fox, proposed a Zone of Destruction and Zone of Survival for Britain. He was taking a somewhat provocative stance in saying that the recovery of the pattern of settlement of pre-Saxon societies in Britain is something that archaeologists cannot achieve. The geographical techniques which archaeologists borrowed from geography to study settlement patterns did not work for prehistoric Britain because we cannot ever know what the total pattern was; therefore we do not know if what we have recovered is 1 per cent or 99 per cent of what was originally there. Except in the Fens in East Anglia, which have been shown to contain the near complete Romano-British pattern, Taylor argues that the prehistoric pattern is never obtainable. Survey work since 1970 has considerably enhanced our understanding of the prehistoric settlement of the British Isles in both the Zone of Destruction (through field investigation, aerial survey and excavation) and the Zone of Survival through terrestrial and aerial survey as well as excavation.

This recent survey work has gone a long way to redress the balance of information; more often than not the archaeological distribution map of settlements tells us two things:

1. Archaeologists have surveyed an area, i.e. the picture we have is not a true one of where people lived but a reflection of where surveys have taken place.

2 *The division between the Highland and Lowland zones of Britain.* After Fox, *Personality of Britain*

2. The validity of the results is further reduced because they are also a reflection of the extent of destruction (or masking) since prehistory. A good example is the belief that the majority of settlement in Wessex was on the tops of the downland, the valley bottoms being devoid of archaeological remains. This has been shown to be incorrect and much of the early activity has been masked by soil movement off the tops and into the valley bottoms, sometimes with over 2m (6ft) of soil (**25**).

13

From this discussion it is clear that every site exists within a landscape, but how do we define landscape? As a tract of countryside on which is inscribed the palimpsest of marks left by different generations of human activity? The emphasis is on the landscape as the countryside and *not* the marks which are left upon it. This is a fundamental part of understanding prehistoric settlements, that the landscape setting has changed in the course of prehistoric time; it is also important to attempt to understand how and when these changes to the landscape occurred.

Recent research work by the author in the northern part of Cumbria began by finding out where the sites were; this was done using a combination of documentary research, field visits and aerial photographs. The difficulty lay in understanding their location in a landscape context, and this involved finding out what date they were and discerning the changes to the landscape in that time span. To understand prehistory it is important to appreciate the time depth; the span of this book is over 8,000 years, or 200 generations (if a generation is taken at 40 years); anyone who has studied history, especially family history, will appreciate what 200 generations represents.

Why are archaeologists obsessed by time and chronologies? In prehistory we want to know the age of a settlement to the nearest 200 years (or perhaps 100 years by the late Iron Age). Three of the sites excavated in Cumbria ranged in date from 3400 BC (**24**) through to 500 BC (**5**) to AD 100 (± 150-200 years). Occupation in this instance has been going on for over 5,500 years and probably continuously, although settlements in the Bronze Age are hard to find in this part of Cumbria. For the interested layman or student of a local area the location of sites was in part determined by the fluctuating sea-levels which we know had risen and fallen in the past 5,500 years.

Archaeologists used to try to define 'prehistoric cultures' as if they would conform to a network of peoples across the British Isles. This has now gone out of fashion because so many new scientific and theoretical avenues of research have opened up. With the increase in excavations and study of material from excavations (especially environmental information which tells us about the climate, flora and fauna of the past), it is becoming increasingly clear that broad generalisations about prehistoric settlement throughout the whole of Britain do not stand up to scrutiny when examined at the local and regional level. Similarly, the large-scale climatic changes are only part of the much more important local shifts in weather. These local changes, both human and natural, are becoming the focus of much archaeological research; the question which needs to be answered is why certain groups of people adopt certain behavioural characteristics and others do not, and how far these groups can be called cultures.

Richard Bradley warns that 'prehistorians pay too high a price when they screen out so much local variation'. Is this local variation a 'cultural difference'? If so, how do we define prehistoric cultures? Prehistorians infer a relationship between the material objects and human behaviour. 'Prehistory is an anonymous study: reconstruction of prehistoric cultures depends on a knowledge of the relationship that exists between material objects and human behaviour in living cultures' (Glyn Daniel, *Idea of Prehistory*). This 'knowledge of the relationship' has been called into question and forms an important part of current research. It does, however, make prehistory a subjective study and one which has to cope with the study of change through time, and the diachronic perspective makes it an exciting challenge.

The use of 'theoretical models' is one way in which order can be obtained; the models are not static neither are they the truth. Any model is an interpretation and attempt at reconstruction and therefore if some of the building blocks are changed, a new radiocarbon date for example, the model will have to be rebuilt. This process of continuous re-assessment is at times frustrating, but it also ensures that the subject never stands still; re-interpretation of archaeological sites is one theme which will be returned to throughout the book.

The title of this book is very similar to Richard Bradley's *The Prehistoric Settlement of Britain* and it might be argued that he said all that can be said on the subject. However, the intervening 25 years has seen a large amount of new material; the basics are of course the same, but the work which has taken place at sites which he mentions as 'work in progress' has now been published and new sites are being discovered and worked on (for example Somerset Levels and Flag Fen). More recently there have been a number of landscape surveys which have led to targeted excavations, for example on Bodmin Moor and in the Vale of Pickering (at West Heslerton). New techniques which were in their infancy in 1978 are now standard practice (for example dendrochronology). There has been a shift away from trying to define prehistoric cultures and a move towards finding and trying to understand prehistoric land-use and landscapes.

It is not always the best way to conduct research to extract one aspect of life (settlement) from the whole gamut of human existence; however, it can be justified if an attempt is made to promote the study of that element because it has been neglected for so many years. An alternative title might have been 'Prehistoric Landscapes' because the interconnection between all aspects of prehistoric life could have been examined more closely, but by focusing on the settlement aspect of prehistoric landscapes it has been possible to show the diversity of settlement types and locations.

Death has been the main focus of so much prehistory, and it has captured the public's imagination on occasion (interest in the Lindow Man, a bog body from Cheshire, led to the TV series *Meet the Ancestors*). Discovering and understanding settlements does not have the same immediate appeal but the question 'where did they live' is one of the most frequent questions that archaeologists are asked.

All those connected with archaeology feel a responsibility towards the sites and landscapes which they encounter; either to preserve them for posterity or if this is not possible to record as much as possible about the site prior to destruction. Similarly landowners, farmers and everyone who visits sites also have a responsibility, akin to a steward, to maintain sites so that they do not become damaged or littered with unwanted material. The sites and landscapes mentioned in this book are often in private ownership; a good way to see most of these is from the air, which only requires permission from air traffic! Visiting the sites on the ground requires permission from the landowner and this is the best way to fully appreciate sites.

I have tried to find a balance between representing sites and landscapes which can be visited or at least 'experienced' and those which are no more than archaeological records as they have been destroyed, are situated on private land or only show as cropmarks. Too often knowledge is trapped in too few places; often these are public places but the vast majority of the public are not aware that these archaeological sites exist. There is a changing attitude amongst professional archaeologists (myself included) that archaeology belongs to everyone (and not just the boffins). This book is offered in the hope that it may bring more information about sites to a wider audience.

2

DISCOVERY AND DATING

The first question posed in the introduction was 'where are the prehistoric settlements?' Imagine a map of Britain with no archaeological information on it; how do archaeologists obtain the information to fill the map up? The purpose of this chapter is to show how the map can be filled up with information relating to prehistoric settlements, from single find spots to whole landscapes. As mentioned in the last chapter this is not the true settlement pattern of prehistoric settlements but the current state of knowledge, and therefore almost certainly not representative (**3**).

To provide an adequate answer to this question we have to look at where sites are, how archaeologists have discovered them, and why there are blank areas. More often than not the distribution of archaeological sites is as much a reflection of survey techniques and recovery strategies as a reflection of past human land-use and settlement (**3**). There are, however, a number of notable exceptions and the more comprehensive the archaeological surveys of Britain become the greater our understanding of prehistoric (and later) settlement and society will be.

The work of antiquarians is an important element in the development of the current picture of prehistoric sites and settlement. The very visible, and in some ways understandable sites, especially Bronze Age round barrows, were the focus of antiquarian attention; the campaigns of Mortimer and Greenwell in the nineteenth century, to name but two barrow diggers, meant that barrows and not the settlement evidence were seen as representative of prehistoric society.

Camden's *Britannia*, published initially in 1587, and later in a number of editions, is the first attempt to describe the antiquities of Britain. This approach, to list all sites and monuments, is still very much with us today; records are kept within each county and for each country in National Monument Records (see below).

In the 1695 edition of Camden's *Britannia* (a translation from Latin) there is scant mention of what happened before the Romans arrived and the little

3 *Distribution of prehistoric settlements in England, from information supplied by the NMR.* Copyright English Heritage

attention it receives is shrouded in biblical and classical references. If we look at Dartmoor, an area now known as one of the richest archaeological areas in the country, Camden says only that there was a forest there. Gibson, who translated *Britannia* adds that, 'The river Dert first runneth thro' Dertmore, a large forest 20 miles long and 14 broad. It was first made a Forest by K. John and had anciently in it many tinn-works. It now yields pasture every summer to near 100,000 sheep.'

This illustrates two crucial points: the first is that the landscape is ever-changing in terms of its appearance, even over a few centuries. Secondly archaeological interpretations change with each generation; we like to imagine that our latest data, ideas and theories are the best yet, but only time can prove us right or wrong. New information and intellectual fashions will change the way we perceive the past in the future.

It was not until William Stukeley (1687-1765) that prehistory received some attention; the main theme of his work was the pre-Roman period. Stuart Piggot, an authority on Stukeley, writes: 'After his death in 1765 we have to wait until the nineteenth century before we can find men taking up the tradition of archaeological fieldwork where he left it, and until the twentieth century before the worth of his work was realised.'

The antiquarian beginnings, although providing a nucleus of information on which we can build, also provided archaeology with some of its techniques of analysis – pottery typologies, relative chronological sequences and an approach to comprehensive cover of the whole country. Admittedly, they were dealing with a much smaller sample, there were few excavations and no crop mark sites, but the idea of making a record for the whole country was prevalent in the late sixteenth and early seventeenth centuries.

The work of the antiquarians during the seventeenth, eighteenth and nineteenth centuries, in terms of excavations and 'surveys' began to bear fruit in the twentieth century with the establishment of archaeology as a subject in its own right. Universities began to teach it and in 1908 survey bodies for England, Scotland and Wales were established with the grand titles of Royal Commissions for the Ancient and Historical Monuments (the addresses are listed at the back of the book). The relevance here is that they provide a national database from which to extract information at a national level. For example in England there are 4,302 records for prehistoric settlements (3) in the national record; in Scotland, the Royal Commission's National Archaeological Record contains 2,202 records for prehistoric settlements with perhaps a further 1,000 records which could be included in any corpus on the subject. The purpose of presenting these figures is to show that we have information about thousands of sites, often no more than a location, a few finds and perhaps an aerial photograph. What we are lacking, for the most part, is a comprehensive understanding of the date and function of these sites. Very few prehistoric settlements have been excavated when taken as a percentage of the whole, and even fewer under research conditions.

At a more detailed level every county in England has a Sites and Monuments Record (SMR) from which information on a particular site can be obtained. Wales and Scotland have similar arrangements which are more regionally based, whereas in Northern Ireland the records are held centrally. The Republic of Ireland, through its Office of Public Works, has recently finished a County by County Register of all sites. These records, at national and local level, are the up-to-date equivalents of Camden's *Britannia* and are invaluable resources for any student of archaeology.

The information contained within these records is a result of years of the accumulation of information from all possible sources; the major primary source was the Ordnance Survey Archaeology Division records; this Division was set up by one of the pioneers of archaeological field survey, O.G.S Crawford, in 1920. Ordnance Survey maps are an invaluable resource (4) for prehistoric settlement archaeology. Although some well-preserved sites are depicted, the value of the maps lies in the topographical information about a site or an area.

One example is the Solway Plain, Cumbria, where the known crop mark and earthwork sites which were thought to be Roman or later left the author wondering where the prehistoric settlement sites could have been. Analysis of the First Edition Ordnance survey maps showed that about 30 areas of former peat bogs had been drained in the nineteenth and twentieth centuries, and it could be

4 *Map extract showing Antiquities (Map 81 Cheviot). Reproduced from the 1980 Ordnance Survey 1:50,000 Landranger map with the permission of the Controller of Her Majesty's Stationery Office. Crown Copyright*

argued that these areas of bogs were an important resource for prehistoric people. Fieldwork and excavation proved this to be the case as well as dating some of the cropmarks to the prehistoric period (**5** and **colour plate** 2). Recently all the wetlands and peat areas have been subject to surveys as part of a national scheme to improve our knowledge of these fragile and disappearing resources.

Survey techniques

Although excavation has played an important part in revealing prehistoric settlements, it is only after surveys have been carried out that excavation can take place. Archaeological survey has a range of techniques and approaches and is fundamental in any landscape study (see *Unravelling the Landscape* in further reading).

Documentary research

Archaeological survey begins at a desk, searching the literature and maps for any reference to archaeological sites in an area; this may involve making requests to the National Archaeological Record, the local Sites and Monuments Record, the Public Record Office, and libraries to chase up references. For the historical periods documentary research takes on a new meaning as original documents have to be examined, read and understood. In all archaeological survey work it is important to find out the nature of any previous work.

Aerial photographs

All areas of Britain have aerial photographs which are of immense value in discovering and locating archaeological sites. These photographs are of two types – vertical or oblique. Vertical photographs are rarely taken for specifically archaeological purposes, but by chance they contain a wealth of archaeological information.

The largest collection of vertical photography was produced from 1945 to 1948 when the RAF carried out a National Air Survey (partly to keep the pilots occupied after the Second World War). Millions of photographs were taken and stored in London; these are now available for consultation through the relevant national aerial photographic collections and libraries agencies (addresses at the end of the book).

Oblique photographs are held in national and local collections and these have been taken by archaeologists as part of aerial surveys all over Britain. A major source of obliques and verticals is the Cambridge University Committee for Aerial Photography (formerly CUCAP, now the Unit for Landscape Modelling) where a collection of archaeological photographs has been created since 1945 under one of the pioneers of aerial photography, Professor J.K. St Joseph. Readers interested in examining their local area can contact these organisations with requests to look at the available photography.

5 *Swarthy Hill, Cumbria. A triple-ditch Iron Age hillfort overlooking the Solway Firth on a sand-cliff.* Crown Copyright

6 *Section through an ancient ditch showing the taller growth of the crop above the ditch.*
Photograph copyright of Aerial Archaeology Publications: Derek Edwards

The purpose of archaeological aerial survey is to locate sites which only show from the air and to record sites and buildings which can be recorded to their best advantage from the air. Many textbooks describe the techniques of aerial photography (see further reading), but the phenomenon of cropmarks should be explained as so many prehistoric settlements are revealed in this way (**6** & **7**). Where a ditch has been dug and subsequently filled up, the ditch fill will hold more water and nutrients than the surrounding soil. The crop above the ditch will grow taller and ripen later than the crop surrounding it; when this is viewed from the air it usually shows as a greener or darker mark in the field and the size and shape of sites can be recorded (**6, 7** and **colour plates 1** & **2**)

Serendipity, luck and the weather play an enormous part in archaeological research, and this is especially true for aerial photography. The dry summers of 1949, 1959, 1975, 1976, 1984, 1989, 1990, 1992, 1995 and 1996 allowed for the discoveries of thousands of new sites. But this is not a new phenomenon; in *Pre-historic Times* Lubbock wrote about the year 1853:

> In consequence of the extraordinary dryness and coldness of the weather during the winter months of 1853, the rivers of Switzerland did not receive their usual supplies, and the water table in the lakes fell much below its ordinary level, so that, in some places, a broad strand was left uncovered along the margin. In this margin 'specimens of human workmanship' were discovered; this was the beginning of the study of 'Lake Dwellings', prehistoric villages situated on the edge of lakes. This Swiss work was to inspire Munro to survey the Scottish lochs and tarns and led to the discovery of a new settlement site type the 'crannog' [see below].

As a result of nearly a century of aerial photography in Britain there are now many projects using air photo interpretation, mapping and landscape archaeology to improve our understanding of human settlement and land use. English Heritage runs a National Mapping Programme (NMP) which relies on access to all available aerial photographs. Using trained interpreters the results of NMP are beginning to transform our understanding of population densities and sizes, especially in the prehistoric period, but this shall be discussed further in due course.

In the twenty-first century it should come as no surprise that new techniques are becoming available to archaeologists. Not only are high quality satellite images becoming more accessible, and less expensive, there are other forms of remote sensors, suitable for airborne platforms. Multi-spectral sensors (which record wavelengths of light not detectable by the human eye) are now being used but perhaps the one with most potential is Lidar. This is a laser beam sensor which emits laser beams from the air to the ground surface and creates an image of that surface (be it trees, buildings, grass, crops or bare soil). The results for

7 *Representation of the way in which sites silt up, become levelled and are ultimately revealed as cropmarks.* Copyright: West Yorkshire Archaeology Service. Drawn by Angela Grove

archaeology, although still being evaluated, are beginning to show great potential in that this method does not rely on any particular lighting or ground conditions.

Fieldwork

The weather has as much to do with archaeological discoveries as good organisation and research designs. Less dependent on chance, but still subject to the vagaries of the weather, are the techniques which involve what has become known as field survey, examining sites on the ground, through fieldwalking (traversing ploughed fields to collect artefacts) or using surveying equipment (theodolites, more modern instruments which electronically measure distances and now global positioning systems (GPS)) to make detailed plans of archaeological sites, and to interpret these remains using all available information (**8**).

Another aspect of field survey, is the use of geophysical measuring equipment (magnetometers and resistivity machines) – often referred to as remote sensing. These machines measure differences of magnetism or electrical resistance in the soil; where the soil has been disturbed the magnetism and the electrical resistance has changed and these changes can be detected (**72, 77, 92, 93 & 94**).

It is also possible to measure the differences in the geochemistry of the soil; for example an area high in phosphates might be one where intense domestic occupation has taken place or where cattle have been quartered. Measuring for these traces is highly labour-intensive but can yield some interesting results.

8 *Maiden Castle Iron Age hillfort, Dorset. The hilltop was first used in the Neolithic period and the slight remains of the long barrow and causewayed camp are just visible. In contrast the massive ramparts are some of the most impressive in England.* Crown Copyright

Excavation

Finally small-scale excavation plays an important part in discovering and understanding prehistoric sites. Often the most detailed field survey, using all the techniques above, can record the site but it cannot give a date or any insight into its function. Small-scale excavation can provide a date for a site be it from radiocarbon or from artefacts discovered during the excavations. To quote from a recent newsletter of the Prehistoric Society (PAST), Professor Barry Cunliffe reported on the Danebury Environs Project (this after 20 seasons at the Danebury hillfort): 'What is clear is that a comparatively small intervention in the field, so long as it is guided by a carefully framed research design and pre-informed by high quality air-photographs and magnetometer surveys, can be extremely productive of new information. At this rate . . . our preconceptions of First-millennium society are likely to change quite significantly.'

Dating

There are two ways in which archaeological material can be dated. The first is by relative means, that is, by association with artefacts dated on typological series. The second is by absolute dating, using scientific techniques such as radiocarbon dating and dendrochronology.

Relative dating methods

Before absolute dating methods had been discovered the only means of dating a site, be it a small enclosure or a large city, was by relative dating. On an excavation the sequence of occupation can be determined by the stratigraphic relationship between the various layers and features. Similarly the artefacts which are excavated can be placed in a typological series, often showing the development of a pottery style, or metalwork style. Typology can give a sequence of events but rarely, unless the artefacts can be linked with historical dates, can it give an absolute date. The sequence is relative to other sequences and its true beginning and end could often only be guessed at unless it can be tied to a known historical event from written sources. In prehistoric Britain this is hardly ever the case as writing was not common until the late Iron Age.

Absolute dating methods

Perhaps the greatest advance in archaeology this century was the discovery of the radiocarbon dating technique in 1958. As with all new discoveries there was a period of euphoria and expectation that this new technique would answer all the dating problems in archaeology. Scientists were aware that there was something not quite right with radiocarbon dating, especially when dating artefacts of a known historical date. It was not until dendrochronology, as a technique, had been developed that the full impact of radiocarbon could be realised.

Radiocarbon dating is possible because the radioactive carbon atoms in all organic material decay at a known rate; this 'half-life', used to calculate a radiocarbon result, is the Libby half-life of 5,568 years (Libby discovered radiocarbon dating). Radiocarbon years are given in uncalibrated years BP, where 0 BP is defined as AD 1950. The error term, ±, should be quoted to 1 sigma (68 per cent chance of being correct). Results and error terms are rounded to the nearest 10 radiocarbon years for error terms of greater than ± 50 years, and to the nearest five if smaller. Recently a new technique for measuring the amount of radioactive carbon, called accelerator mass spectrometry (AMS), has been developed. By this method, the number or a proportion of the number of C14 atoms is measured in the sample relative to the C13 and C12 atoms. This adds to the accuracy of the technique.

The major assumption of radiocarbon dating was that the background radiation in the atmosphere, throughout prehistoric (and historic) time, was constant. This assumption was found to be correct until artefacts of a known historical date were radiocarbon dated, and the discovery of a complementary and equally important technique, dendrochronology.

Dendrochronology is the dating of wooden artefacts and trees through the patterning of tree-rings. This enabled samples of wood of a known date (via dendrochronology, see below) to be radiocarbon dated; a calibration curve was created against which 'radiocarbon years' could be calibrated against real years (**9**). The final limitation to radiocarbon dating was the age of artefacts it could date; given the half-life decay of carbon there had to be a limit on the very old things that radiocarbon could date; this limit is approximately 50,000 years.

Dendrochronology was developed for climatological studies and is based on the knowledge that trees produce an annual growth ring but that the distance between

9 *The radiocarbon calibration curve*

10 *A dendrochronological sequence*

each ring is not constant; the growth each year depends on the climate (sunshine, rainfall and temperature). Thus, the pattern of rings for a tree's life will be similar to other trees in the same area or of the same date (**10**). A databank now exists from the present day going back 8,000 years matching up the various patterns and sequences of tree rings. The discovery of long-lived trees in the Californian desert (bristle-cone pine, *Pinus aristata*) enables the sequence of patterns to be stretched back to about 8,000 years (about 7,000 for oaks, *Quercus* sp.).

Without radiocarbon, dendrochronology would be an enormous advance in itself but could only be used where wood had been preserved. Coupled with radiocarbon dating however it enabled the calibration of the absolute tree-ring date to the radiocarbon date to be made. This inevitably showed that the amount of radiocarbon in the atmosphere was not constant and that at certain times there was considerable change in radioactive levels. Two high-precision laboratories (Belfast and Seattle), using different conventional radiocarbon techniques and different tree species, have independently produced curves which agree across a number of 20-year time spans. Belfast has produced a calibration curve going back to 5210 BC. The calibration of radiocarbon dates is a science in itself, but simply put the advent of dendrochronology has made the radiocarbon dates too young. Any calibration curve may have a wiggle which is pronounced enough to allow two possible dates for any single charcoal sample. Thus for any one sample it is possible to have at least two dates. This often means that radiocarbon dates are quoted as 2337-2360 or 2232-2349, as possible dates.

Radiocarbon dates are published in many different ways; as calibrated dates (BC) or if they have not been calibrated, by using the bc or bp convention which denotes radiocarbon years before Christ or before present. All radiocarbon dates are published with 'standard deviations'. The deviation is the range in which the date is likely to fall and the confidence level is the statistical confidence we can have in the date falling within that range. Radiocarbon dating is based on probability theory; there is either a 68 per cent chance, one standard deviation, to determine the age or there is a larger time band at the 95 per cent level, or two standard deviations.

The archaeological journal *Antiquity* uses the agreed 1986 standard and the lower case bp for uncalibrated dates and small BP for calibrated dates. Some authors use the convention RCY (radiocarbon years) after a date; others use 'cal BP' for calibrated and small capitals BP for uncal. In 1993 a new calibration curve was introduced and the editor of *Antiquity* suggested new conventions; c14 for radiocarbon, TL for thermoluminescence date and UTh for uranium/thorium dates. The presentation of radiocarbon dates is confusing; my only advice is handle all dates with care looking for a BC, bc or BP, bp and if the dates are uncalibrated or calibrated. In this book I have had to use the dates which have been published; so some are calibrated and some not.

There are other absolute dating techniques, such as potassium–argon dating, which can date objects or rocks that are older than radiocarbon methods allow. Similarly uranium series dating can date objects of a few hundred to 500,000 years ago. New techniques have also been developed for luminescence dating; any crystalline minerals in natural or man-made objects, which have been heated, can be dated by recording the light emitted by electrons when the material is re-heated under laboratory conditions. This technology has now been extended to unburnt soils (known as optical dating) which have been exposed to sunlight and then re-buried. This is a very useful technique for dating sites where artefacts or other forms of dating are absent.

Environmental studies

One important advance in the natural sciences within the last 50 years has been the way in which soil and sediments can be analysed; the aim of the analysis is to find what is contained within the archaeological deposits which is not

11 *Pollen diagram, from Barfield Tarn, Cumbria*

12 *Barfield Tarn from the air; tarns and bogs provide good sediments for studying past climatic changes.*
Copyright R. Bewley

immediately visible to the naked eye. By studying the microscopic and macroscopic remains in sediments, the details of the site formation processes mentioned in the introduction can be better understood. Techniques of flotation (washing soil in water and skimming off the material which floats) have been developed so that small fragments of bone, seeds and macrofossils can be identified. Similarly, sampling strategies have been developed for pollen analysis.

The study of pollen grains (palynology) was developed by a Swede, Lennart van Post, in 1916, initially for forest trees but as the techniques developed it helped to identify all pollen-liberating vegetation. Large numbers of pollen grains are suspended in the atmosphere and will be preserved when deposited in anaerobic conditions (peat deposits especially). If soil samples of archaeological or palaeoenvironmental deposits are taken and examined through a microscope the identification of the pollen grains can indicate the different types of vegetation (especially trees) which had been growing at or near that particular place. The samples are taken throughout the stratigraphic sequence of a site or peat bog and thus a 'history' of the vegetation at that site can be presented from the pollen evidence (**11** & **12**).

One episode on an European scale which pollen analysis has identified was the 'Elm decline' at about 3000 bc; there have been numerous debates over what caused this widespread decline in elm. Was it as a result of prehistoric clearances for settlements and fields? Was it the dreaded elm-beetle which carried a disease which killed the elms? Was it a climatic change which affected elms? The answer has to be a combination of all three but it is unlikely that elms were selected for clearing when there was a rich variety of trees; the arguments for selective use of elm leaves for fodder will be considered later.

Larger macrofossils are also isolated from the archaeological deposits so that studies of seeds and insects can be made. These analyses inform us about the types of crop grown (if any), the insects which lived there and the microfauna (small animals) which fed off the debris left by prehistoric peoples. Insects can be good indicators of climate; a good example is the work in the Somerset Levels where the studies of beetles informs us about the climate of the period and complement the pollen and plant macro-studies. Dung beetles are good indicators of large herbivore activity.

If we return to the blank map of what is now the British Isles and take it back to 12000 BC, the present east coast does not exist and the British Isles are part of the European continent (**13**). By about 6000 BC the sea-level rose to cut off the land bridge and form the North Sea. The rise in sea-level was due, in part, to melting ice but also to the dipping of the land; the west and north of the British Isles was (and still is) rising whilst the south and east are sinking. This has implications for the discovery of sites before the land bridge was closed; many Mesolithic sites are under the North Sea. The occupants of many of these sites will have travelled to the North York Moors and all along the current east coast of England. Thus, the sites which we do find in these areas are only a small part of the total picture. It is unlikely we will ever be able to completely excavate one of the sea-bed sites, though more are being discovered and recorded.

There are a number of ways in which we can conceive the past; one is through supposed cultural groupings – cultures like the Halstatt or La Tène; or we can use the technological classifications of stone (Palaeolithic, Mesolithic and Neolithic), bronze (Bronze Age) and iron (Iron Age). Alternatively, we can use the environmental distinctions as in **Table 1**. These are based on vegetational

13 *Reconstruction of the land bridge with the European mainland after 7000 BC. The British Isles have been rising in the north-west and sinking in the south-east since the end of the last glaciation*

Table 1 Vegetational Zones
of the Late and Post Glacial

bc	Name	Zone	Vegetation
12,000			
	Older Dryas	I	Park tundra
10,000			
	Allerod interstadial	II	Birch with park tundra
8,800			
	Younger Dryas	III	Park tundra
8300			
	Pre-Boreal	IV	Birch, Pine forest
7600			
	Early Boreal	V	Hazel, Birch, Pine
7000	Later Boreal	VI	Hazel, Pine a) Elm, Hazel b) Oak, Elm c) Oak, Elm, Lime
5,500			
	Atlantic	VIIa	Mixed Oak Forest. Alder, Oak, Elm,Lime
3000			
	Sub-Boreal	VIIb	Alder, Oak, Lime. Elm decline.
500			
	Sub-Atlantic	VIIc	Alder, Oak, Birch

and climatic changes which took place and have names or Roman numerals to distinguish them.

The technological terms – Mesolithic, Neolithic, Bronze Age, Iron Age – are used here as a loose framework on which to hang 8,000 years of prehistory. It is widely recognised that they are as meaningless as referring to the late twentieth century as the 'computer age' or 'car age' but they have gained such wide acceptance they are useful labels. The changes in technology did not denote dramatic and instant cultural changes; through the long periods of prehistory cultural changes took place, and these are reflected to some degree in prehistoric settlements.

Defining what we mean by 'prehistoric cultures' is an interesting subject and the difficulty of studying human behaviour is the extent to which our 'material culture' (pottery, personal objects, houses, tools, prestige objects, arms, etc.) reflects the 'tribe' or group to which we belong, if indeed these objects reflect this at all. Archaeologists attempt to extract *meaning* from artefacts, houses and burials and the significance of the deposition of any object; this is the goal of our investigations into past human behaviour but there are no definitive answers, only speculation, and this is what makes the subject so intriguing.

3

THE EARLY YEARS

What do we mean by settlements? Is it a term for the individual settlement (including the houses and ancillary buildings) or is it the areas or landscapes in which prehistoric people settled and lived? I have interpreted it as a combination of both; that is the landscapes in which people have lived and also, where necessary, a detailed analysis is presented of those few settlements which we know about. This has opened the way to mentioning sites and types of sites which may not be settlements in the strict sense but often prehistoric settlement areas are defined not by the discoveries of houses but by the distribution of non-settlement information (burial cairns for example). Especially for early prehistory it is necessary to take a broad view.

As we saw in the previous chapter, since the nineteenth-century archaeology has been helped (and hindered) by Montelius' Three Age System – Stone Age, Bronze Age and Iron Age. This system has been a useful framework for conceptualising the past as a system of progress from stone technologies to the metalwork of later periods. It is embedded in the belief that technology is the motivating force of progress and that time inevitably means progress. The fact that we use word-processors and drive around in sophisticated pieces of machinery does not mean we have 'progressed' as a civilisation; it simply means we think we have greater control over our lives than was the case in prehistory.

In the early post-glacial years, survival in a new and changing environment was the challenge which faced the colonisers from the south and east. The picture which I would like to portray is how people lived. The starting point will be the arrival of new settlers once the final ice (at least until the next Ice Age) had retreated, and finish with the arrival of the Romans. The introduction of different technologies does not in itself affect the settlement pattern distribution and therefore the changes which took place in prehistory throughout Britain, in terms of settlement, will be dealt with chronologically. This has its problems in that the Mesolithic in southern England can be seen to end in the fifth millennium BC but in parts of northern England and Scotland carried on into the third millennium BC or later. Generalisations are difficult to sustain and each area or region should be examined in greater depth than I have been able to delve.

It is worth stressing that life in earlier prehistoric times was very different from today; it was not, as the nineteenth-century writers would have us believe, a time of wild barbarians and savages. The people, *Homo sapiens sapiens*, were the same as we are today. The difference was that their everyday life was almost completely involved in their own survival. Finding, killing, gathering and obtaining food and shelter were the daily priorities; in fact it is no different today except that we receive money to do a particular job or task and pay someone else to kill the animals, collect the vegetables, build and heat the house. The use of fire was a long-established skill and must have played an important part in daily life. The popularity of camping today is perhaps in part due to the 'back-to-nature' desire many people have; if you examine the spacing of tents and caravans in a field it gives an insight into the way people will 'occupy' an area.

The backdrop for prehistoric settlements is the landscape of Britain after the retreat of the glaciers (15,000-12,000 BC) and after the country had been re-settled. The return of *Homo sapiens sapiens* was accompanied by herds of elk, reindeer, horse and red deer with the demise of larger mammals such as mammoth, bison, woolly rhinoceros, elk and lion. The retreat of the ice and the colonisation of new faunal and floral species happened over a period of a few thousand years; not least because of the fluctuations in the re-advances and retreats of the ice between 15,000 and 10,000 BC. The important point is that, once the various animal and plant species had established themselves, there began a period of occupation in the British Isles which has remained uninterrupted since. The only major change during the last 12,000 years has been the separation of the British Isles from the continent in about 6000 BC (**13**), a break which has now been joined by the Channel Tunnel. Vive l'Europe!

The first phase of settlement has left little trace and is a continuation of a Palaeolithic way of life based on hunting and gathering. The main focus for settlement may have been caves but there were also 'open' sites; these sites are much harder to find than caves and we have a distorted picture of Palaeolithic life in Europe. Caves and a number of occupation sequences from this period have been discovered; not surprisingly the caves of south-west England, Wales and the Mendips were occupied first. However, the north was also colonised, at Victoria Cave in North Yorkshire and Kirkhead Cave in southern Cumbria. There can be no doubt that other sites from the early recolonisation period will be found, not least the 'open' sites in low-lying areas. Many of these will be under the North Sea and the Channel and are therefore well protected from the archaeologists' intentions to excavate them (if not protected from dredging and fishing activities), but further research on this type of site would shed light on these early settlers.

The Mesolithic

By about 8000 BC the population had expanded sufficiently and so open sites in a variety of locations were being established. Other changes had taken place as the climate ameliorated, notably the growth of woodland; the pine and birch woodland which provided suitable habitats for the wild ox, red deer, roe deer and wild pig were exploited. Similarly, the retreat of the ice left a landscape which is hard to imagine today, but one which contained many areas of open water. The Lake District is a good example in England, and the lochs and loughs of Scotland, Wales and Ireland, as all the water in these lakes and upland tarns is a remnant of the last glaciation.

Sometimes the smaller lowland tarns survive today (**12**) but generally they have become overgrown with peat and are either bogs, or have been drained and are now part of the agricultural landscape. These areas of open water were numerous and not always large but they were the local resource centre – the supermarket of the Stone Age. Around them, the animals and birds would congregate for water, food and fish (as happens today) and as the human race is essentially lazy (or will take the most effective course of action in the short term) the easiest place to hunt and fish would be around these tarns and lakes (except when at the coast). Fish, as a resource for these hunter-gatherers (fishing is a combination of both hunting and gathering), has been much underrated and the survival of many of the early prehistoric communities depended on freshwater and marine resources.

At one site, Culver Well, in Portland, Dorset, a large shell midden with lean-to shelters, has had over 16,000lb of shell excavated. It has been estimated that this is the equivalent of 2,550,000 calories; given that a family of eight requires about 17,400 per day there would have been enough calories for 150 days. The excavated part of the midden only represents one-fortieth of the site. Thus, our concepts about mobile hunter-gatherer populations has to be revised when sites such as these are excavated. John Wymer, a leading authority on the Mesolithic period, quotes some similarly interesting statistics on the enormous waste of a shellfish diet; it has been estimated that one red-deer carcass is the equivalent in food values to 52,267 oysters. Apparently 700 oysters would have to be eaten every day, in the absence of any other food, yet only 1,400 cockles or 400 limpets provide the daily nutritional needs. The further away one gets from written history the more one has to rely on abstract statistics and extrapolations to attempt to understand prehistoric society. Fish, in contrast to shellfish, are highly nutritious, and easily obtainable. The many coastal Mesolithic communities will have caught and eaten salmon, sea trout and whole variety of other fish, the remains of which are unlikely to have survived, given their fragile nature.

Archaeologists refer to the people at this time as *hunter-gatherers* as they did not farm or grow crops or keep animals. They collected food by hunting animals, fishing and gathering wild fruits, nuts and any edible plants. The name also gives an indication of the type of settlement which they may have used. That so few hunter-gatherer (Mesolithic) sites have been found should be no surprise (**14**). From the end of the Palaeolithic period and well into the Neolithic period this way of life was the predominant mode. It leaves little trace except for the stone tools and only exceptional evidence of settlement and houses. Evidence from Mesolithic sites comes from middens, bones, flint artefacts or flint scatter sites, with the occasional use of caves for a variety of purposes including cooking and burial.

Not surprisingly the coast played an important part in the settlement pattern of hunters and gatherers from 8000 to 4000 BC. The sea-level was much lower than today, from 52-36m (170-120ft) lower from 7000 to 5000 BC (**13**); at 5000 BC the sea-level stabilised at a similar level to the present day. Many early

14 *Distribution of Mesolithic sites in Britain.* Sources: various

Mesolithic sites are now submerged in the east of the country but can be found on the 25ft (8m) contour in the west.

There are a number of dated sites from the coast in the Atlantic period when the climate was on average 2°C warmer; although this is not a great fluctuation in climate it is enough to make a significant difference for habitation in upland areas. From the distribution map (**14**) the dispersed settlement pattern can be seen but this is not a true reflection of the settlement pattern; too many factors do not allow us to recover a representative pattern as yet.

Territorial analysis

It is possible to model the pattern at a local level with the use of 'site catchment analysis'. Site catchments are defined as a specific area around a site; the area can be defined in terms of time or distance from a base camp (for example) to a hunting site; usually for early prehistoric sites the definitions are 10km (6-mile) and 5km (3-mile) zones, or the length of time estimated it would take to travel these distances. A modern analogy would be the siting of supermarkets on the edge of towns; their location is determined by a number of factors but the proximity of a large population within easy reach of the shops (usually on a well-used route) is fundamental for the shopper and supermarket itself.

Hunter-gatherer activities can be seen as dispersed within a widening zone of concentric circles within a catchment zone, centred around a focal point. The 'activity dispersal zones' would have overlapped as no activities are wholly mutually exclusive, and indeed the sites need not be. The use of sites at different seasons for different purposes (hunting, base camp, killing, flint knapping etc.) was obviously important, and a model has been proposed for these early hunter–gatherer societies (**15**).

15 *Model of Mesolithic settlement* After S. Palmer, T. Darvill and A. Whittle

16 *Excavations at
Oronsay.* Courtesy
of Paul Mellars

One of the most well-known excavated sites is that of Oronsay (**16**). Oronsay
is a small island of 14km² (5.8 sq. miles) in the Inner Hebrides – 30km (19 miles)
west of Scottish mainland at 56° North. The site consists of six shell middens –
three of which had been identified in the nineteenth century and excavated
between 1879 and 1913; the other three were identified in a programme of work
undertaken by Paul Mellars from 1970. In all, it is a unique site in the British
Isles. Five midden sites around the coast of Oronsay were excavated – answers
were sought to a number of questions: was the island occupied continuously by
a small resident population or was it an intermittent pattern of occupation by a
variety of more mobile wide-ranging groups who were based on neighbouring
islands or the mainland? Could such a small unit have survived as a breeding unit?
What determined the choice of specific locations? Why were the 'sites' re-
occupied and re-used so specifically? Can we view five midden sites as
'occupation sites' in the usually accepted sense, or are they more like extraction
areas where shellfish were processed at this central point? There is some evidence
for hearths and hut structures at one midden site, Cnoc Coig. The shell middens
were used over a relatively long time span, 700-800 years from *c.*5000 to 4200
BC, and then came to an abrupt end.

It is interesting that in the Mesolithic period the archaeological evidence
consists of middens and flint scatters. Shell middens are often the most
informative type of site as they are the 'rubbish' from settlements which
informs us what people ate and what they threw away. Many settlements, as
found by archaeologists, are just pale reflections of what actually took place on
the sites. To understand human behaviour we have to study 'rubbish'.

Rubbish and middens

There is a project in the United States (and now, Britain) which started life as
the Tuscon Garbage Project. The American archaeologist who started this,

William Rathje, now studies the modern 'land-fill' sites to inform local authorities on what is being thrown away and the effects of land fill deposition on certain objects. Coupled with this research was a series of interviews with the local population to find out what they thought they 'consumed' and what they actually threw away. This work has helped our understanding of any anthropological study – what people actually do and what they say they do are two very different matters. For example, if a man was asked how much beer he had consumed the amount was exaggerated; if a woman was asked about her male partner's beer consumption the figure would be less than what was actually found in terms of cans of beer in the rubbish bin. Similarly in a meat shortage in one area of America the amount of meat which was discarded (past its sell-by date) increased rather than decreased; people were hoarding meat and thus exacerbated the meat shortage!

Shell middens are therefore important as Mesolithic settlement evidence because they are the rubbish from a settlement. So what were they eating? Fish and shellfish in varying proportions were an important part of the diet; the percentage varied at Oronsay between the middens but shellfish was the predominant food, with the consumption of fish up to 65 per cent in one phase of one midden.

At another well-known Scottish site at Morton in Fife near the mouth of the River Tay, occupied from 4300-5300 bc, the occupants had a much more varied diet; they hunted red and roe deer, aurochs and pig, and also ate whelks and mussels. Seabirds were also caught (and probably eaten) as were some deep-sea fish, like cod and sturgeon, which would have required a boat. The occupation at this site was spread over a large area and there is evidence for living structures, hearths and flintworking.

Most archaeological descriptions of the Mesolithic concentrate on the different stone tool technologies and not the people nor the landscape they occupied. The inland sites do not often contain the organic remains which the coastal sites do and we have to rely on the stone technologies.

What the stone tools tell us is that in the eighth millennium BC people lived by hunting a wide range of forest animals such as red and roe deer, pig, elk and aurochs with bows and arrows. There is also evidence that they trapped beaver, pine marten, wild cat and badger.

One area which has attracted much work on the Mesolithic sites has been the North York Moors and this is a good illustration not only of what there is to be learned about the early colonisation of post-glacial Britain but also of the biases which our methods of working impose on our understanding of the period.

We have already seen general models for the way they located their sites and Jacobi's model, below, emphasises the mobility and seasonality of sites. The area we today call the North York Moors is interesting in the Mesolithic period; its proximity to the east coast means that it was probably exploited to a greater degree for longer in the Mesolithic than any other upland area. If we remember the land-bridge with Europe (**13**), the population in the catchment area would have been large and it exploited this upland area for hunting. In northern England a number of types of site have been identified:

a) seasonal sites, summer or winter hunting;
b) winter sites in lowland – Vale of Pickering, the Fylde, the Isle of Axholme and also along the Trent itself;
c) summer sites in North York Moors or Pennines.

Each community is estimated to have been perhaps 25 people or more.

Starr Carr

This model can be supported by the original interpretation of the most famous of all British Mesolithic sites, Starr Carr, where excavations lasted from 1949 to 1951. Starr Carr is situated in the low-lying Vale of Pickering only 8km (5 miles) south-west of Scarborough; the Vale is bordered north and south by higher ground; the North York Moors to the north and the chalk Wolds to the south.

The stone tool evidence suggests that 60 per cent of the retouched pieces at Starr Carr are end scrapers and burins (that is, they were used for the processing of skins) whereas the higher sites in the North York Moors (**17**) contained different assemblages; more archery-type artefacts.

As mentioned earlier, faunal remains are used to confirm or deny the interpretations from other sources. In the excavations at Starr Carr, the excavator, Professor Sir Grahame Clark, was interested in (amongst other things) the time of year when the site had been occupied. He felt that the faunal assemblage (the bones of animals left behind) would give him this information. The bone report concluded that the site had been occupied from October to April i.e. autumn to spring; the evidence for this was the red deer skulls discovered at the site with antlers attached. As red deer shed their antlers in April the assumption was that the deer were hunted in the winter. As a result of this interpretation the site was seen as a winter base camp, occupied in the eighth millennium bc; one radiocarbon date for the site is 7,538 bc.

The site of Starr Carr is one of the fixed points of British archaeology – every student has to know about it and as a consequence it has been re-interpreted at least nine times. The re-interpretations started with the excavator himself; again with the subject of seasonality as a major concern he was able to reinforce his model of migration of deer and humans from the winter base at Starr Carr to the summer ranges of the North York Moors, the chalk Wolds to the south and even west to the Pennines. The other re-interpretations, from 1978 to 1988, suggested that the site of Starr Carr was important not for red deer as meat resource but as raw material (antler) and that is was a *kill site* used all year round, or an industrial working site, the availability of water being important for soaking skins; or that the red deer migration theory did not work and the site was occupied in the early summer or all summer, or that the lack of fish, especially pike, was not a winter indicator as Clark suggested but was a result of the rivers not yet being colonised; finally another interpretation has the site as a base camp on the wide range of mammalian species and artefacts.

This confusing list is presented here to highlight the widely differing interpretations that can be assigned to one very important and well-excavated site. The number of re-interpretations inspired Tony Legge and Peter Rowley-Conwy to 'revisit' the faunal assemblage of Starr Carr and their latest, and perhaps not final interpretation is at least based on a complete re-assessment of the bones. Legge and Rowley-Conwy conclude that:

a) the site was used only in late spring and summer;
b) the red and roe deer animals were culled when they were either one or three years old;
c) there was less meat available than originally estimated and therefore a reduction in the scale of occupation is necessary;
d) the site was possibly a hunting camp, with the meat being removed to a base camp elsewhere.

In the space of 35 years the site of Starr Carr, the most famous of all Mesolithic sites, has gone from being a winter base camp to a summer hunting site – all based on the same evidence. This example is not meant to criticise in any way the scholars involved in the debate on Starr Carr, it is meant to serve as an example of how archaeology operates. There is no final answer, as there might be in mathematics, because the evidence is open to interpretation. Starr Carr was the forerunner of many future excavations in terms of the technique of excavation and presentation of the environmental and faunal data. New questions about faunal assemblages have risen since 1954 and it was inevitable the early excavation results would be reassessed. A recurrent theme throughout this book is the way in which reinterpretations of sites add to their interest and are part of how we come to know what we do about prehistory.

One of the questions which archaeologists ask of a bone assemblage is 'which bones survive?' Is it only the long bones for meat or are the bones a representative sample of the whole carcass? (It has to be remembered that the thinner, more fragile bones do not survive to the same extent as the thicker bones like the femur and astragalus.) Having answered these questions it is possible to obtain the minimum number of individual animals (MNI) at any site. In doing these analyses the faunal experts can make an assessment of whether a site was a 'kill' site or a consumer site and also at what time of year the site was in use. By analysing the fracturing of the bones it is possible to say whether the bones were gnawed by other animals (dogs in particular) or were consumed by humans.

Pattern of settlement

Where does this leave our understanding of eighth- to sixth-millennium archaeology? We still know that the predominant form of obtaining food was from hunting, fishing and gathering and that the whole of the British Isles (before it was separated from Europe in about 6000 BC) was occupied by a mobile population who made use of all types of resources from the sea to the uplands and also the lowlands. The problem is one of discovery; so many of the sites are probably under the North Sea or buried beneath subsequent peat growth. The discovery of sites from this period has depended largely on former antiquarian interest and now local amateur interest, and on the local weathering of the sites from buried peat. The good survival of flint means that one aspect of the Mesolithic is over-represented in the archaeological record and the evidence of settlement, organic material, is rarely found. The brushwood platform at Starr Carr is one of the very few organic finds from this period.

The pattern of settlement is more a reflection of recovery techniques than it is a pattern of human settlement. The upland sites are generally situated on the tops of ridges and valley heads, overlooking natural basins where the movement of deer can be watched. There is evidence that forest trees above 350m (1150ft) were burnt down to keep the view clear. A drawing (rock art) from Cueva de los Caballos (Spain) shows 12 hunters with eight beaters driving a herd of deer towards the archers. This can be interpreted as a summer hunt as there are females and fawns and only one stag; the stags normally arrive in October for the rut.

There can be no doubt that rivers were important for the communities that depended on natural resources. The problem we have is finding the sites which were near rivers 8,000 years ago. The water-drainage patterns were different from today, especially as the major rivers were still developing. At the micro-scale, we need to look at the river bank and stream edges which were the edges then; in a few cases (for example in Teesdale) there are Mesolithic deposits eroding out of the existing river bank, but these instances are rare. There is a current excavation (2003) on Exmoor led by Paula Gardiner of Bristol University which is situated at the springhead (Hawkecombe Head) and is producing evidence of hunting and knapping (using material from Porlock beach). The ever-changing course of the rivers means that tracing the original course is the first task and looking for the sites the secondary. If we add to this the mobility of these people, lowland communities might have had 'territories' or catchment areas of up to 80km (50 miles), the difficulty of establishing the Mesolithic settlement pattern can be appreciated.

17 *Location map of Starr Carr and the Mesolithic sites in the North York Moors. a = Maglemosian microliths; b = Maglemosian axe; c = Maglemosian bone point; d = Sauveterrian microliths, two reconstructed in worden half*

Estimating the total population of the British Isles in the Mesolithic is clearly difficult but it has been estimated at about 20,000 people, which is on the conservative side. There are few burials to help with identifying what the people looked like and what differences there might have been between communities in burying their dead.

If we conceive of the first phase of post-glacial colonisation as that from the retreat of the glaciers to the removal of the land bridge with Europe (6000 BC), it helps to place in context the changes which happened after 6000 BC. During this first phase the sea-level had been rising as the ice was melting. This rise in sea-level meant that communities would be exploring new areas for colonisation as their normal hunting and fishing grounds were being removed by the sea. Therefore, they began to expand further north in England and into Scotland. From 6000 BC onwards, because Britain became an island, the developments in technology are not affected by contacts across the land bridge with Europe. The flint technology changed to a smaller, geometric microlithic assemblage, possibly as part of a change in the types of missiles which were used. The woodland environment changed too with a more closed woodland, with oak, alder, lime and elm taking over from pine and birch.

It is logical to assume that the population density increased as the area available for settlement was reduced and, therefore, more communities further north are found after the land bridge had been closed. Similarly, a wider range of resources was used which in itself would have brought about changes in technology.

Forest clearance by the mid-fifth millennium was beginning to affect soil and soil degradation; felling an oak, which can hold and use several gallons of water a day, taking it up through the roots and losing it via its leaf system (transpiration), will affect the groundwater. Waterlogging can occur in cleared areas and the growth of peat has been shown to begin about 5500 BC at Kinder Scout in the southern Pennines. Woodland clearance was a process which went on for over 8,000 years and its effects have to be emphasised (**18**). Once trees have been felled the soil and groundwater properties change, and soil erosion is much more likely to occur. Environmental studies have shown the effect of human intervention in the uplands especially; when this is coupled with the climatic changes it is easy to see why the uplands are not the same as they were even 3,000 years ago.

So far I have dealt with settlements as concepts, as part of the settlement system rather than as the places themselves. As has already been mentioned, the sites are often near water, be it a stream, river or the coast. The majority of sites in the Mesolithic are on sandy soils and many of the sites mentioned are base camps from which foraging for food and hunting would have taken place. Very few structures, which might be termed dwellings, from this period have been found but hearths are common on most sites and, although tent-like structures would leave little trace, it is likely that tents made of animal skins sewn together were the normal form of house. Modern nomads use similar tents which are easily collapsible.

Dense forest of pine, birch, hazel and oak.   Grazing by animals, some forest clearance.   Hunters' camps, burning of trees.

Shrubs and trees cleared, more animals, less regeneration.   Land clear, soil degradation.   Partial reforestation.

18 *Model for clearance of woodland.* After Simmons

At most sites which have been excavated there are remnants of stake holes and post-holes, but it is difficult to interpret these as anything more than tent-like structures. At one site, Broom Hill, Braishfield, near Romsey in Hampshire, a series of post and stake holes surrounds an artificial hollow in which there was a central post and internal hearth; this is one of the most convincing Mesolithic houses ever to be found (**19**). Near Dunbar on the east coast of Scotland a circular hut, 4.8m (16ft) in diameter was discovered; the excavators claim it is the oldest house in Britain, populated by toolmakers if the 30,000 pieces of flint are any indication of activity. The hut was probably a tent-like structure and had a central hearth, but had been burnt to the ground leaving only charred evidence.

The reconstruction (**colour plate 4**) summarises much of what is known about the Mesolithic settlements. A small group of tents and an associated structure for drying fish and hides would have been situated in a forest clearance with easy access for water. The bow and arrow was an essential everyday weapon and woodworking (centre foreground) an important task for making arrows and boats (middle right). Deer, birds and the sea also played an important part in early post-glacial life. John Wymer in his Shire Archaeology publication on Mesolithic Britain paints a positive picture of life in a Mesolithic settlement. 'The camp would have been a busy place, when fully occupied, with old equipment being repaired and new being made. Ethnographic parallels suggest that the people would have entertained themselves with story-telling, music, singing and dancing.' We know very little about their customs (marriage ceremonies, birth and death rituals).

In the Test Valley in Hampshire, a Mesolithic site, Bowmans Farm (which was excavated in ten days because of the pressure of the pipeline construction),

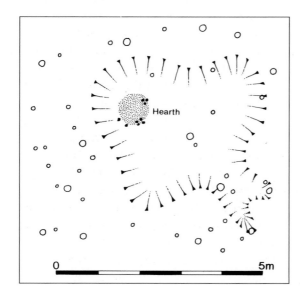

19 *Broomhill, one of the few structures from the Mesolithic period.* After Wymer

was situated on the edge of flood plain of the River Blackwater. The flint from the site is late Mesolithic or even transitional Neolithic. A preliminary radiocarbon date of 4800 BC fits in well with the lithic material.

The four houses found during top-soil clearing constituted two pairs of shallow ring ditches, one pair 25m (82ft) apart and the other 10m (32ft) apart. The ring slots were filled with large quantities of charcoal. The entrances were to the south-south-east and the fourth house was more sub-rectangular than circular. The topsoil was only 30cm (1ft) in depth and had it been ploughed regularly, it would have been destroyed (and was not likely to have shown as a cropmark). Wood from the site has been identified as oak, willow, poplar, birch and buckthorn; hazel is attested from the nuts found. These species would have provided adequate building material for post and wattles. From the analysis of the carbonised deposits there is some evidence for seasonal activity.

The discovery of this highlights one of the ways in which new material is brought to light; the local Sites and Monuments Record (SMR) was asked for information in this area and it was shown to be 'archaeologically blank'; given currently available information, the pipeline in this area did not seem to be damaging any archaeology. Fortunately, the whole length of the pipeline was archaeologically evaluated once the topsoil had been stripped (as fieldwalking would have revealed little). It was during topsoil stripping that the site was found.

It is worth stressing that the information contained within any recording system is the current state of knowledge and not confirmation of the presence or absence of sites; surveys and evaluations have to be done continuously if we are not to lose unrecorded archaeological information.

If this hunter-gather way of life was so successful why did it change? Why should these communities change from semi-mobile groups with a good resource base and develop farming practices? Was it population pressure or growth, was it external contacts? It is now a well-established fact that farming (growing crops and husbanding livestock) spread from the Near East, where the wild progenitors of the cereal plants lived, which were to form the basis of the new economy (20). The causes (and effects) of the spread of farming have been the subject of many books and there is one fundamental point worthy of discussion which has changed over the past twenty years. When the spread of farming had become understood as a phenomenon, theories about the changes it brought were developed. Initially it was argued that farming produced sedentary population and 'surplus labour' and therefore, there was the possibility for building large monuments (henges, long barrows, causewayed camps, stone circles and avenues for example). However, anthropological research was also beginning to show that the first affluent societies were the hunter-gatherers or foragers; they had time on their hands too, even if they were supposedly 'mobile' populations. More recently the opposite argument is being made that it was the building of the monuments, by semi-mobile populations, which brought about a social change and it was as a

20 *The spread of farming into Europe.* After Clark

result of the monument building that these populations took up farming and 'settled' in purpose-built settlements. Whatever the answer, change did take place, but how did it manifest in terms of human settlement?

By the end of the fifth millennium the population was becoming larger and forming tribes (probably) with exchange mechanisms. Then, in the fourth millennium, the pace of changes accelerated with the introduction of agriculture. Not surprisingly this had an enormous and profound affect on the landscape and 'prehistoric settlements'. It is possible that the effect of the arrival of farming has been overstated, especially in the Neolithic and Bronze Age. Ideas and models about pastoralism and pastoralists are in the doldrums and much of archaeological thought and theory is often as a result of modern intellectual fashion (currently involving structuralism, postmodernism, processual and post-processual archaeology); but pastoralism is perhaps staging a comeback as more evidence comes to light of a combination of herding and crop cultivation from the Neolithic onwards.

In the Mesolithic – or the 'bit after the glaciers but before farming' – it is easier to talk about individual sites (as there are relatively few of them) and at the same time begin to understand something of the changing landscape of the time.

However, the changes in the landscape are not reflected by changes in technology. Similarly, a change in technology does not necessarily herald a change in economy, land-use or settlement pattern. There may be other forces at work which will have affected the decision-making of prehistoric people be they hunter-gatherers, proto-farmers or nomadic pastoralists. In terms of understanding prehistoric settlements through time it is instructive to look at a number of landscapes and see how they were used from the Neolithic to the end of the Iron Age.

4

NEOLITHIC SETTLEMENT
AND EARLY FARMERS

Towards the end of the fifth millennium BC a combination of factors led to the adoption of farming and a reduction in the hunter-gatherer way of life. For a considerable period of time, into the second millennium BC and in some cases even into the first millennium BC, prehistoric communities in the British Isles did not rely solely on farming; with abundant natural resources there was no need to. The adoption of farming techniques and processes took place at different places and at different rates during the fifth and fourth millennia (from about 4300 to 3500 BC).

The transition from hunter-gatherer to farmer took place over a large area (from the Near-East to Britain, from northern Europe to the Mediterranean) and not all at one time (**20**). Detecting the transition in the archaeological record is virtually impossible; gradually we see indicators of a more settled way of life, with the construction of large monuments which have survived several thousand years. This so-called 'Neolithic Revolution' is more of a transition than a revolution in the modern sense of the word. There can be no doubt that the former hunter-gatherer way of life had been overturned but it did not happen overnight and the evidence from early Neolithic Britain suggests a combination of settled farming with a mixture of hunting and gathering. The crucial question is how this change manifests itself in the archaeological record in terms of settlement sites.

This is difficult to answer if we are looking for villages or hamlets of Neolithic farmers. We need to approach the subject in terms of understanding the way in which Neolithic people used their landscape; if we do that then we can place the sites we know to be Neolithic in a comprehensible context. Recently, there has been a re-thinking of the nature of the Neolithic. Some European sites which were thought to be Neolithic settlements in fact turned out to be burials or sites similar to causewayed enclosures. This has produced theories which suggest that the large monuments of the period, the long barrows, causewayed enclosures and megaliths, were not so much the products of farming communities with a settled lifestyle, but monuments in a landscape which were important places for a more mobile, hunter–gather style society. However, more recent evidence has come to light which supports the model of a Neolithic society in which houses, often very well constructed with large oak posts, were important in terms of domestic life and are used by scholars today in support of the view that these were agricultural communities, living in one place and not on the move.

In theoretical terms we may have come full circle, and perhaps even found a middle way, in that the evidence for the development of the farming from the Near East and across Europe is so strong it is unlikely not to have spread into Britain at much the same time. The models of diffusion and migration, so popular in the early part of the twentieth century, have not been fashionable for a long time. Yet now they are becoming debated again as the events in modern Europe and the Middle East have shown that large scale movements of people are easily triggered by political events (the ending of the Cold War and its consequences).

To illustrate the Neolithic way of life, there are many examples to choose and one of the best is the Somerset Levels which shows the way in which one type of landscape was used at this time. Having done this, the picture will be broadened to include 'causewayed camps', then the evidence for individual houses will be looked at, followed by a few known Neolithic settlements from Orkney to Cornwall.

The wets and wood

The story of the Somerset Levels in prehistory and the way in which sites were discovered has been fully told in *Sweet Track to Glastonbury* by John Coles and Bryony Coles, published in 1986. The reader is urged to consult this book for a greater understanding of the way in which prehistorians can provide answers to the fundamental questions of who was living when and where.

The authors of that book freely admit that they do not know where all the people lived, or what the size of the settlements were (although other areas help us to answers these questions). However, by using the evidence from the Sweet Track, a Neolithic trackway across a watery, boggy area of what is now a peat area, we can deduce the following facts about the Neolithic people (**21**).

The wood for the trackway can be seen to have been felled in one single year, in the winter of 3806/7 BC. (This is an absolute date, based on dendrochronology.) The conversion of the trunks into planks must have taken place immediately as the roundwood (for pegs and rails) was cut to length and sharpened before it was seasoned. It has been estimated that enough wood was prepared for 6,000 pegs, 2,000m of rails and 400m of planking. There was a large variety of species of wood, over a dozen, from two different woodlands, one to the north and one to the south. It has been suggested that this represented two families (or groups of adults) working at two locations. We can therefore suggest at least two settlements, one to the north and one to the south of the low-lying areas.

From the evidence of woodland management these groups had been living in the area for at least a generation; the hazel tree-ring evidence points to this, as does the fact that some of the ash used in the Sweet Track had been felled at least 30 years before the track was constructed. The people using the trackways stayed for about 10 years; the track was repaired for up to 10 years after it had been built. The track became engulfed in the peat during the third millennium, which has preserved it for 5,000 years.

Normally we would label the people living in and around the Somerset Levels (and other similar areas) 'farmers', but we must not think of them as farmers in the modern sense of the word. They 'farmed' some parts of the land and were probably more settled than the communities living 500 or more years before. The evidence for them being farmers is slight indeed and with the natural resources which the Levels would have provided, the need for farming was not great. Why grow crops when you can obtain a plentiful supply (and variety) of food from the back garden? There is some pollen evidence from the Westhay area to suggest that some cereal was grown and that the forests were

21 *The Sweet Track, a wooden trackway 5,800 years old.* Somerset Levels Project

cleared. It is not absolutely certain that the builders of the trackways were farmers. That they also enjoyed hunting is proven by the Meare Heath bow (**22**). They were also affluent (by Neolithic standards), leaving fine pottery behind and one finely made jadeite axe. These artefacts also suggest that they had good external contacts; perhaps indicative of a highly mobile society which had its base around the Levels.

The Sweet Track (named after Ray Sweet, the local person who discovered it) is not unique. There are many more tracks; another one being Garvin's brushwood track built about 2400 bc (or 3000 BC after calibration).

One feature of Neolithic society was its mobility and the differences from region to region. It is perhaps in the nature of our own society that we want to understand 'cultures' or 'society' as some sort of homogeneous entity. This is to impose our twenty-first century ideas and cultural thinking on a population which thrived 5,000 years ago.

The settlements of the builders of the Sweet Track and Garvin's brushwood track in the Somerset Levels may well have been hamlets with houses made of wood; we know they were skilled carpenters. Yet, if the settlements were located on the higher, drier ground to the north and south, the wood would

22 *A reconstruction of the Meare Heath Bow, made of yew with probable decorative binding.* Somerset Levels Projects, Drawn by M. Rouillard

not have survived and we have to remain thankful that the last trace of their manipulation of the area, the trackways, have survived.

In other parts of the country we have not been so lucky, but a rare example of a Neolithic settlement is Ehenside Tarn, Cumbria discovered and 'excavated' in the 1870s; the artefacts which were discovered there (**23**) are still some of the finest wooden objects from the Neolithic times. This site consisted of a series hearths around what must have been a lake or tarn (cf. Barfield Tarn). The tarn had filled up and become a peat-bog which the farmer decided to drain in 1869. During these drainage works a number of Neolithic polished stone axes and wooden artefacts were discovered (**23**). This site still represents the best Neolithic site in the area in terms of preservation; yet it can only have been a settlement for one or two families. The evidence for a large Neolithic population in the area is based on finds of Group VI axes (from the Langdale Axe factory, **colour plate 4**). The distribution of stone axes throughout the area was interesting but not indicative of a large settled population. The axes which have been found and recorded were either from the small glacial ridges which are a common feature in the area (up to 25m (76ft) above OD) or were found near bogs or tarns. A distribution of the bogs

23 *Wooden artefacts from Ehenside Tarn, Cumbria.* NB original from *Archaeologia* 1874 44

51

in the area taken from the First Edition Ordnance Survey map, has over 30 bogs in 700 square miles (1,800km²), which shows that mobile groups would have a plentiful supply of fish, birds and game which would inhabit these areas. Given the proximity of the sea, marine resources were important throughout the Mesolithic and no doubt the Neolithic as well.

Similar to the use of the Brue valley in the Somerset Levels these Neolithic people were using the local resources for their food supply, as much if not more, than farming. The settlement pattern for this area of Cumbria, the Solway Plain, was likely to have been small groups of highly mobile people moving throughout the area with contacts beyond; perhaps stationary for a summer or two, but certainly not sedentary and chopping down trees (particularly elm) as clearance areas for their farms.

Interestingly one site, a D-shaped enclosure showing only as a cropmark site, was excavated and despite an expected Iron Age date, produced three Neolithic radiocarbon dates, which when calibrated are early Neolithic *c.*3400 BC (**24**). The function of this site is, however, unknown but in its construction large oak timbers were used; so far it is unique in the area. It can be argued that the location of any site is important in terms of its 'catchment', or territory. This has led to a large body of literature on 'site catchment analysis' and I maintain that this site, Plasketlands, is a settlement. Its proximity to the sea, as mentioned above, has to be as important as its location on fertile sandy soils and a high and dry position.

The elm decline

Relevant here is a discussion of the cause of the 'elm decline' at *c.*3000 bc. This is a good example of the way ideas change within a generation as well

24 *Plasketlands, Cumbria. A Neolithic site discovered by aerial photography and excavated by the author.* Crown Copyright

as being a watershed in prehistory. Pollen studies began to show throughout Europe that at about 3000 bc there was a definite decline in one particular tree, elm. One study in 1966 argued strongly for an anthropogenic (man-made) cause for the elm-decline in northern Cumbria. If this was the case there should be good evidence for the Neolithic settlements in the area. To affect the tree population to the extent that it can be recorded in the remains of tree pollen is no mean feat. So, where were all the Neolithic sites? Is the elm decline man-made or does it have another cause? The recent (1980s) elm decline was caused by an elm disease (a microscopic fungus, *Ceratocystis ulmi*) which is transmitted by two bark beetles (*Scolytus scolytus* and *S. multistriatus*). In light of this, Oliver Rackham has proposed an interesting alternative cause to the elm decline. The elm species has been subject to a series of declines since records began and he postulates that the beetle which transmits the disease could have been active as long ago as the Neolithic. It is partly coincidental with the population expansion during the Neolithic that the decline took place *c*.3000 bc.

A further argument against an anthropogenic cause is that elm declines more than any other species; if prehistoric communities were clearing woodland, or managing woodland, this clearance would not been so species-specific. This is despite the theory that in Denmark cattle were fed on elm leaves, and therefore their use as fodder aided their decline; this is a questionable proposition on the grounds that the population of cattle to consume these leaves would have been enormous and the human population needed to eat the cattle would also have been far greater than all estimates suggest. Also, if elm trees are your main source of food for cattle, you would surely wish to maintain them and not let them decline.

This discussion is relevant in that it highlights the interrelated nature of many disciplines which aid archaeologists in their interpretations. Archaeology has to seek assistance from other sciences to corroborate, or refute, the information it derives from survey and excavation. A good example of this is the evidence from beetle remains found in samples of peat taken from around the Sweet Track. Five of the species identified are no longer found in Britain and four may have become extinct (in Britain) because of climatic change. When the distribution of these four (*Oodes gracilis*, *Chlaenius sulcicolis*, *Anthicus gracilis* and *Airaphilus elongatus*) was examined it showed that they favoured a more continental climate perhaps with winters 2-4°C colder and summers 2-3°C warmer.

Causewayed camps

Let us now turn from landscapes where Neolithic populations were known to have settled but for which details of individual settlements is limited, and

25 *Distribution of aerial photographs held in the national Monuments Record, England.*
Copyright English Heritage

concentrate on the beginnings of 'enclosures', or as a recent book refers to them, the *Creation of Monuments* (see Oswald *et al.* in further reading), a title which is drawn from Richard Bradley's Rhind lectures, published as *Altering the Earth*.

These sites, known as causewayed camps or enclosures, might have no place in a book on prehistoric settlements, as we know they had a variety of functions, but they are too important as a group to leave out when we know so little about their function, and they represent some of the first enclosing activities in the archaeological record.

Any 'enclosing' is a fundamental, social, intellectual and political move that is irreversible. It is also seen first in the interrupted ditches of causewayed camps. Causewayed camps are not in anyway confining, given their size, 1.7–9.6ha (4.2–23.7 acres); but they do represent the first formal enclosure for communal activity. We cannot fit them into a single category – are they settlements, ritual, or burial sites? They are all these and we should try to understand how they operated in Neolithic society. If they are not settlements then they performed an important function as part of the Neolithic landscape and undoubtedly cut across the boundaries between domestic, economic and ritual behaviour which have been so compartmentalised in today's society (**29**).

As a class of site they are one feature of the Neolithic landscape which was not a long barrow, henge, passage grave or monument connected with the burial ritual. Archaeologists have to use labels and names; 'causewayed camp' is so-called because of the encircling ditches having causeways at regular intervals. In the low-lying areas of Britain this type of site has been referred to as an 'interrupted ditch system' (i.d.s. for short). Here I will use the term causewayed camp to include all sites, whether earthworks, stoneworks or cropmarks which have an encircling ditch with causeways within it (**27** and **colour plates** 2 & 7).

This subject and site type is another good example of the continuous re-interpretation of the sites; initially studied by Curwen in the 1930s, as more were discovered, especially through aerial photography (**25**) they were re-analysed in the 1970s by Rog Palmer. Since the first edition of this book (in 1994) there has been a major review of the sites by archaeologists from the former RCHME (now part of English Heritage; see Oswald *et al.* in further reading. Not only have these enclosures been re-evaluated, this renewed interest and expansion of the site-type into hitherto unexplored areas has led to further discoveries of well-preserved examples as earthworks and stoneworks (**colour plates 7, 8 & 9**), bringing the total in England and Wales to 70 sites. During the writing of the first edition there were informal discussions between experts that one of the very few hillforts in Cumbria, Carrock Fell, was not a hillfort at all, but a stone-built causewayed enclosure; it was included as a 'place to visit' but given the uncertainty of its origins, I decided not to use an illustration. Having now revisited the site on the ground and from the air (personally) and as a result of an RCHME survey, we can be much more confident in considering Neolithic origins for this site (**colour plate 8**). There is evidence of later use at the site so excavation alone will prove this interpretation right or wrong.

Rog Palmer, the first person to re-work the original material since Curwen in the 1930s, has shown that there are two 'groups' of causewayed camp – those which mainly survive as earthworks and have widely spaced ditches, either single or multiple ditches, and are all on high or hilltop locations. The other group, by contrast, are low-lying, with closely spaced ditches, perhaps more defensive, and usually on sloping ground near rivers (**29**). This may relate to the function of the sites or it may be that the sites perform a similar function in different locations and it is the location which determines the form of the site. A visit to Windmill Hill (dating to *c.*3600–3300) is instructive in that it does not look like a hill until

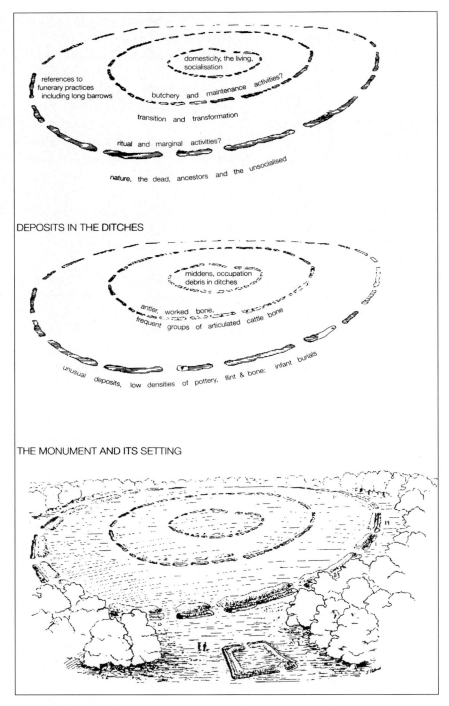

DEPOSITS IN THE DITCHES

THE MONUMENT AND ITS SETTING

26 *Windmill Hill, possible model of the interaction of zones , activities and symbolic significance of deposits.* After Oswald *et al.* 2000 and Whittle and Pollard's original drawing

27 *Reconstruction drawing of the neolithic causewayed enclosure at Staines, Surrey. The image conjures up a meeting place, perhaps for the exchange of livestock and other commodities. The archaeological evidence suggests there was only one entrance and that both circuits were not in use at the same time.* Museum of London

you are standing on top of it (**colour plate 6**). At Windmill Hill sherds of pottery from over 1,300 different pots have been found, with over 95,000 worked pieces of flint, which is indicative of considerable activity. Some of the pots were made over 115 miles away on the Lizard peninsula in Cornwall (or at least that is where the clay came from). Some of the stone axes found there had come from not only Cornwall, but also North Wales and the Lake District. Thus, it was clearly an important meeting place, the high number of cattle bones found suggested to Stuart Piggott (who was one of the first to attempt to study the Neolithic in any depth) that it was a cattle market.

Further analysis of the camps by Palmer divides them into four groups (Midlands, Thames, Scotland, South-west, Sussex) and into two size categories: the smaller from 1.7 to 3.5ha (4.2 –8.6 acres), and the larger 5.5 to 9.6ha (13.5– 28 acres). Groupings were attempted in a variety of ways. Geographical location was a strong indicator but other methods were also employed, such as classifying the sites according to the number and spacing of the enclosing ditches (**28**).

Recent surveys and analysis by Oswald and his colleagues have added to the numbers (up to 70 in all) but have also aimed to re-evaluate the evidence, not using statistical methods but by trying to understand the sites in terms of their 'sense of place'; which is trying to understand how the people in the Neolithic perceived the hills, rivers, trees, forests and clearances in social, economic and ideological terms. This aspect of landscape archaeology has been developed by Chris Tilley in his *Phenomenology of Landscape*.

In examining the sites in terms of their location, four new groupings have been proposed – river valley floor; river valley side; upland: lowland oriented, and upland: upland oriented. The first two categories are self-explanatory but the latter two refer to sites in upland locations but from which only lower land (lowland oriented) or higher land (upland oriented) can be seen. These distinctions do not inform us immediately of the meaning of the sites and the site types but they do open new avenues for research so that specific questions can be asked when any of these sites are investigated further. As an approach it also helps to show that those sites with a number of circuits may have 'grown' over a number of generations, from being a single circuit site to a multiple circuits. Initially the site may have been in a small clearing but the latest addition may have helped the transformation of the site from a hilltop location for one purpose to a much larger meeting place or settlement.

Figure **29** shows the distribution of causewayed enclosures, the majority of which are north of a line from the Humber to the south-west through Staffordshire. This is not an accident of discovery as there has been many years of searching (through aerial photography and other techniques) (**25**) throughout Britain. It is possible further research will widen this distribution.

28 *Four possible groups of Neolithic interrupted ditch systems.* After R. Palmer

From the distribution map it is possible to see a number of interesting aspects, not just the importance of rivers, but some clusters, even groups of sites and in some cases possible pairings. One cluster of particular note is the concentration of five enclosures within 5km of each in the Welland valley, which flows into the Wash. They exhibit very similar characteristics in terms of location, size, shape and the number of circuits. The possible pairings can be examined further but the sites at Birdlip and Crickley Hill, on promontories of the Cotswold scarp, suggest defence was a major factor in their construction.

Oswald *et al.* suggest at least five activities which were carried out in causewayed camps: feasting, exchange and manufacturing, settlement, funerary ritual, and defence. None are mutually exclusive and they highlight that today's distinctions between domestic and ritual behaviour are not transferable to the past. Others have tried to find zones of activity within the sites and this has been summarised (**26**). We have to try to use the limited evidence we have to understand the possible models we have created for these Neolithic sites (**27**).

Another way of grouping these sites has been by examining the pottery styles in the Neolithic. Roger Mercer argues that the pottery styles can be seen to be cultural and that the distribution of pottery production can be divided into four: (i) a south-west group including Cornwall, Devon, Dorset; (ii) a Wessex and west to the Cotswolds group; (iii) a Sussex group; (iv) a central group in the

29 *The distribution of causewayed camps in England.* English Heritage. See Oswald *et al.* 2000

Thames valley, the Chilterns, East Anglia and the east and central Midlands. (There is a fifth group, the northern Grimston-Lyles Hill group, outside the distribution of causewayed camps.) The distribution of these pottery styles is, in certain cases, coincident with the distribution of causewayed camps. More work is needed on this but it is a beginning in terms of groupings, especially when combined with the recent re-examination and some targeted excavations.

The proposal that a particular pottery style is equal to a particular 'cultural group' is questionable but is commonly argued in archaeology. Linking four pottery styles with the tentative results of the four 'causewayed camp groups' is stretching the evidence to the limit. It does, however, produce a hypothesis for further work. It introduces for the first time in prehistoric communities in Britain the suggestion that the population was sufficiently large to have allowed for regional variation and diversity; indeed, as will be shown below, there is strong evidence for conflict between these groups.

The history of causewayed camp studies is interesting from the point of view of demonstrating how archaeologists work and how the subject is always changing. First of all a site is discovered, then a few more, and a label is given to one of them as a group – in the 1680s the classic causewayed camp, Windmill Hill, was referred to as a Roman Camp. Then there is a period of more survey, excavations and research and the 'class' of site gains credibility, in this case 'causewayed camp'. As early as the 1930s Neolithic camps were defined as having certain characteristics: causeways, concentric lines of defence where necessary, following the contour, and situated on prominent hills and ridges. As time has passed many of the sites included in the class have been excluded, so the class is always redefining itself; the need for this is increased by new discoveries, either through fieldwork or more often through aerial photography (**25** and **colour plates 8 & 9**).

We cannot use modern divisions of function and causewayed camps, they could be schools, banks, stock exchanges (in the original sense of the term), law courts, parliaments, barracks, hospitals and homes. It is also worth noting that not all Neolithic enclosures are causewayed (Court Hill, Singleton and Bury Hill, Houghton).

The function of one causewayed camp, Hambledon Hill (**30**), has been argued for after extensive excavation. As we have seen, the act of 'enclosing' was an important development in human history and Roger Mercer argues that this represents a farming economy dominated by cattle herding. Cattle can be seen as a mobile source of wealth which are in need of protection, as well as being kept out of the settlements. If they are a source of wealth they will be coveted by others and in Mercer's words they play a part 'in stimulating easily satisfied greed, [and] feed the notion of intercommunal conflict. Enclosure is a response to these demands.' Hambledon Hill contains a number of enclosures; the earliest is the Stepleton enclosure, which encloses about 1ha (2.4 acres). The evidence that this enclosure was a settlement, some of which had been

30 *Hambledon Hill from the air showing the Iron Age hillfort with earlier long barrows inside it (middle right), and the causewayed camp with the remains of excavations visible as a white patch (middle) and the Stepleton enclosure, which is possibly a Neolithic settlement (top left).* Cambridge University Collection of Air Photographs: copyright reserved

removed by subsequent use of the hilltop, comes from pits with domestic rubbish, broken flint tools, fragments of eroded pottery, fragments of animal bone and carbonised vegetable matter. Included in the organic remains were remnants of emmer, einkorn, barley and one seed of *Vitis vinifera*, domesticated grape, unique in the British Neolithic; perhaps a long–distance import? There is also evidence of an oven, flint and antler workings, plus the remains of a still-born child in the cavity of the wall. All these finds suggest that domestic activity was an important part of the function of the site. However, the bone assemblage suggests feasting rather than careful meat management. Whole articulated joints of meat were partially consumed and then discarded.

Whatever the nature of activity here the defences were enlarged and the top people wanted to remain on top. There was evidence of a conflagration – the recently cut ditches of the larger site were open and clean when fire swept through the site; the wind appears to have been in the north-west and the timber of the rampart burnt and fell into the ditches. Beneath one part of the ramparts, which had collapsed into the ditch, two skeletons were found of men aged 20. One had been shot in the back by an arrow while carrying a young child; he had either fallen or been pushed and this action caused the child to be crushed or at best smothered. The other man had at least been buried but his grave had been back-filled with scorched chalk, probably derived from the rampart debris.

There was obviously a need for defence but why enclose such a large area? The answer may be gained from the animal bone evidence – Tony Legge examined the bone from Hambledon Hill and concluded that the herd was predominantly for milk production with a certain number of cattle reserved for meat consumption. Yet there is no water, so any protection within the enclosure was surely for short-term expediency. The construction of the defences in their final phase may seem a massive investment of labour to counter raids or short-lived warfare; yet it was designed to protect the main food resource.

Hambledon Hill itself encloses over 50ha (123 acres) with partial defences, using a timber-reinforced rampart which was later added to by a double line of outer defences: there were three timber-lined gateways and it has been estimated that over 10,000 timbers were used in the construction of the defences. All of this immense defensive work had been constructed by 2700 bc. This was a huge investment of labour probably for cattle herding, but the lack of water suggests, at least to the excavator, that the site would not have withstood a long siege and therefore, the interpretation of substantial defences were as much a symbol of power as an effective refuge. The evidence suggests that the site was used as a settlement over many centuries.

A site which has been compared with the early phase of Hambledon Hill is Carn Brea south-west of Redruth in Cornwall. The defences of this site encircle two summits and an area of 18ha (46 acres) with two smaller enclosures around the central and eastern summits. The eastern enclosure, contains good settlement evidence, and encloses about 1ha (2.4 acres); its wall is made of massive rocks weighing up to 3 tonnes and joins naturally defensive rocks. Within the enclosure are a number of terraces on which timber houses were built, probably enough for 100-150 people. Apart from the obvious activities of obtaining food through farming (and no doubt cattle played an important part in this), the people were involved in a number of economic activities.

At this time (c.3000 to 2700 bc) the production of polished stone axes was a major industry (not just in Cornwall but throughout Britain); at Carn Brea large amounts of the stone from the Camborne area (Group XVI rock) was worked and polished for the 'trade' in stone axes. The exact mechanics of the trade have not been possible to work out, but it is likely that causewayed camps, large enclosures, and henges were important meeting places, even markets for these sorts of goods. This activity gave the inhabitants of Carn Brea a certain power and status. They were able to import pottery from over 30km (19 miles) away and the chert (a type of flint) from Devon and Dorset. The problem with any power base is that at some point it has to be defended and sustained. The evidence from Carn Brea indicated that it was attacked from all sides by archers (over 800 arrowheads have been found); the walls were slighted and there is evidence of universal burning across the site. The site was not, as far as the excavator can tell, ever re-occupied in the Neolithic. What the cause of this attack was we will never know, but it does highlight the beginning of the tensions between communities once territories and locations are marked out as belonging to one group.

The axe trade also brings us to a site near Honiton in Devon, Hembury, which has Neolithic origins and suffered a similar fate as Carn Brea. Hembury occupies a promontory site and was also occupied in the Iron Age. In the Neolithic the evidence from excavations in the 1930s suggests that the site had been attacked; the ditches had been filled with a mass of burnt material leaving a layer of charcoal no less than 15cm (6 in) thick and in places up to 60cm (2ft) thick. Amongst this burnt debris were 120 leaf-shaped arrowheads. Prior to its destruction, Hembury had been part of a trade network which imported gabbro-gritted pottery from south-west Cornwall, as well as a trade in flint and chert (from Dorset) and stone axes from Cornwall.

Another site where similar events took place is Crickley Hill, near Cheltenham in Gloucestershire; the first occupation on this site was of an oval barrow, but with no burial. The area was subsequently cleared and the ditch of causewayed camp excavated; within the enclosure rectangular houses were found ranging in size from 5m by 2m (15ft by 6ft) to 10m by 5m (30ft by 15ft). It seems that this site too had been attacked by archers. Crickley Hill also attracts attention because of the discovery of what appears to be a 'shrine' – a stone-built platform, the centre of which was kept clean, even though the area around contained 'midden debris'. It is associated with an orthostat. The shrine appears to have been in use long after the site, as a settlement or defensive refuge, had been abandoned.

One aspect of Neolithic sites, causewayed camps in particular, which can be detected throughout prehistory is the tradition of continuity – at at least three sites, Hembury, Maiden Castle and the Trundle, hilltops were used as causewayed camps in the Neolithic and were also used as major strategic defences in the Iron Age.

By contrast, another well-known, but recently discovered and excavated site, is Etton, near Peterborough. Its situation is low-lying in contrast with the sites mentioned above. The site was discovered during the hot summer of 1976 by aerial photography and showed as a very faint cropmark (**31**). The reason for the faint cropmark was that the archaeological features were buried beneath almost

31 *Plan of the causewayed camp at Etton.* After Pryor

a metre of alluvium which had built up over 5,000 years in the Welland valley. The importance of the excavations carried out by Francis Pryor and his team was the discovery of the waterlogged deposits on the site; this has added an enormous amount of information about this type of site, without providing us with any clearer answers! The ditches enclosing the site were cut into the gravel and the material from the ditch spread across the interior of the site; there appears to have been no attempt to build a rampart. There were causeways between the ditches. Each ditch seems to have been open for a relatively short time and were re-cut a total of eight times, probably on a seasonal basis. There is evidence of at least one rectangular structure in the interior.

The results of environmental analysis indicate that cereal was being grown and cattle were once again a dominant part of the economy. Any attempt at reconstructing the way of life of the people as part-time cereal producers with seasonally grazing cattle has to include the 'ritual' aspect of life at the time. Deposits which are not connected with what we know of domestic life have been found. In one ditch terminal there was a deliberate deposit which contained a neatly arranged bundle of meat (only the bone survives), with calf bones and a complete Mildenhall ware bowl. All these were placed on a birch-bark mat. Another section of ditch appears to have been deliberately back-filled with 'deposits' placed within and beneath the back-filling. For example, cremated human bone was placed next to a human skull with an antler 'baton' and a small standing stone nearby. A wooden vessel was also placed near this collection of artefacts. These deposits were obviously important to the people making them and may have had some apotropaic function, but we can only speculate on their significance.

1 *Buckland, Oxfordshire. A recently discovered causewayed camp and associated mortuary enclosures.* Crown Copyright NMR, 4609/21

2 *Cropmarks of a late Iron Age and Romano-British site at Wolsty, Cumbria.* Copyright R. Bewley

3 *Reconstruction of a Mesolithic settlement.* Drawn by Timothy Taylor

4 *Pike O'Stickle, Langdale, Cumbria. An aerial photograph of the Neolithic axe factory.* Copyright R. Bewley

5 *Bodmin Moor, Cornwall. Rough Tor stone-built hillfort as a false colour infra-red aerial photograph.*
Crown Copyright, NMR SX 1480/12/333

6 *Windmill Hill, Neolithic causewayed enclosure.* Crown Copyright, NMR

7 *Neolithic causewayed enclosure at Greenhow, Cumbria, recently discovered as part of English Heritage's aerial reconnaissance surveys.*
Copyright English Heritage

8 *Carrock Fell, Cumbria, prehistoric enclosure.* Copyright R. Bewley

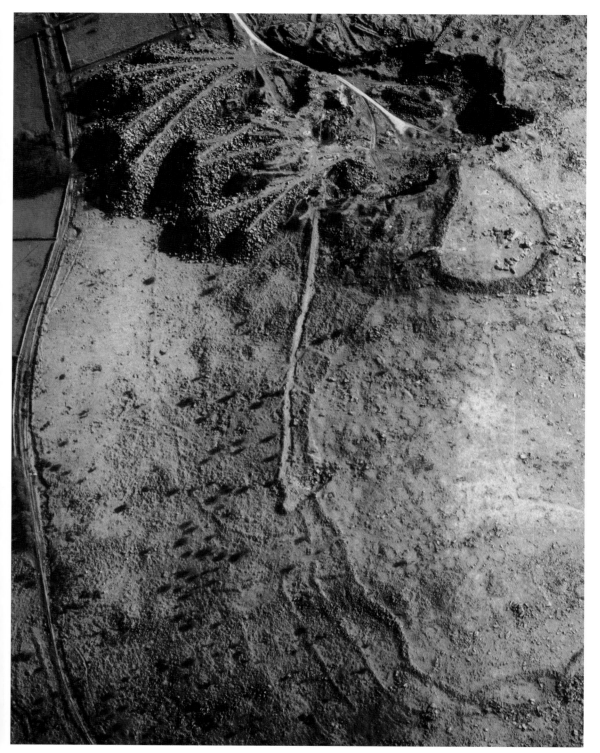

9 *Stowe's Pound, Cornwall. Two stone enclosure encompass Stowe's Hill, a larger one encircling most of the hill top and a smaller one which is adjacent to the more recent quarry. Inside the larger enclosure there are two Bronze Age cairns and a stone round house. Visible on this false colour infra-red aerial photograph are a number of circular platforms (where stone has been cleared for wooden houses). It is likely that this site is of a similar date to Rough Tor, late Neolithic or Bronze Age.* Crown Copyright, NMR SX 2572/20/24

10 *Aerial photograph of the reconstruction of the Bronze Age settlement at Flag Fen, Cambridgeshire. Note the Roman road running south from the site, showing as a pale line.* Crown Copyright, NMR 4238/14

11 *Reconstruction of an Iron Age hillfort.* Drawn by Timothy Taylor

12 *Aerial photograph of a low-lying Iron Age hillfort at Wardy Hill, Cambridgeshire. Note the developed entrance features.* Photograph by Ben Robinson

13 *A 'banjo' type enclosure with trackway and funnel entrance and associated curvilinear and rectilinear sites at Ashton Keynes, Wiltshire.* Crown Copyright, NMR 4604/7

14 *Butser Hill Ancient Farm, Hampshire. Butser Ancient Farm is an open air research laboratory which is researching the domestic and agricultural life of the Celtic Iron Age. It is the only place in western Europe where ancient livestock, cereals and plants can be seen in the context of the fences, fields and domestic dwellings and buildings of the Iron Age. The studies at Butser also include industrial processes such as pottery and iron manufacture as well as charcoal burning. To begin to understand what prehistoric life was like a visit to Butser is essential. See section on places to visit.* Copyright Peter Reynolds

15 *Reconstruction of the Iron Age settlement (c.200 AD) at Thorpe Thewles.* Copyright Cleveland County Archaeology

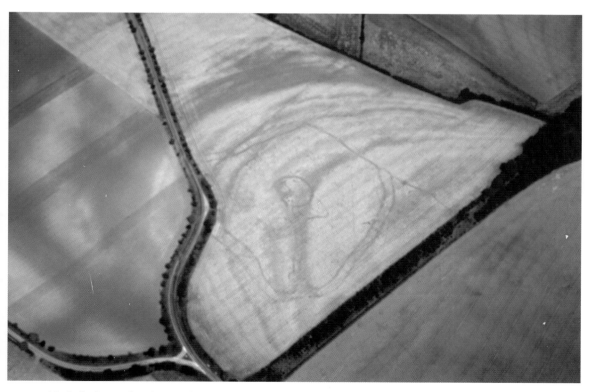

16 *Rollright Heath, a banjo enclosure with surrounding ditches.* Crown Copyright, NMR

17 *Distribution of banjo enclosures in North Oxfordshire.* Copyright English Heritage

18 *Distribution and location of banjos in the Lambourn Downs.* Copyright English Heritage

ploughsoil

ploughsoil

19 *Formation of Cropmarks.* Copyright English Heritage

20 *Reconstruction of the Iron Age settlement at Chysauster, Cornwall and its surrounding landscape.*
Drawn by Judith Dobie. Copyright English Heritage

21 *Reconstruction of a house and courtyard at Chysauster.* Drawn by Judith Dobie. Copyright English Heritage

22 *Broch of Gurness, Orkney. Broch and later surrounding settlement.* Copyright R. Bewley

23 *Glastonbury lake village from the air in 1966.* Photograph by Jim Hancock

24 *Ingleborough hillfort, North Yorkshire, in the snow.* Crown Copyright, NMR

25 *Uffington Castle and White Horse Hill, Oxfordshire. The significant topographical feaures and hill-top location of the hillfort and chalk-cut prehistoric horse are clearly visible in the aerial view.* Copyright R. Bewley

26 *A prehistoric settlement on the edge of Brothers Water in the Lake District, near Hartsop Hall. The large upright stones appear to mark an entrance to this low-lying settlement.* Copyright R. Bewley

27 *Dyke Hills, Oxfordshire. An important defended settlement at the confluence of the River Thames and River Thame. The defensive earthwork connects the two rivers, enclosing c.114 acres. It is probably a late Iron Age* oppidum. Crown Copyright, NMR SU 5793/74

These sites and discoveries highlight on the one hand how little we know of the nature of Neolithic settlement, and on the other the variety and complexity of society 5,000 years ago. There are many ritual aspects to these sites; to have excluded them would have been to reinforce our own concepts of what is domestic, economic, and ritual or spiritual. Any distinction between these aspects of life is a false one as we all have everyday rituals, which may be mundane but to the archaeologist or anthropologist may have some significance. If we cast our net slightly wider for a moment and look at Neolithic towns, even cities, in Turkey the combination of home and shrine, or Do-It-Yourself divinity is evident. At Çatal Hüyük in Anatolia there is a Neolithic mud-brick city, where the rectangular houses (with a floor area of about $25m^2$, $135ft^2$) are interspersed with shrines in considerable numbers; although the shrines themselves are special places. Throughout history this is not an uncommon practice: the Romans had household gods and shrines as well as external temples.

Neolithic houses

The evidence for Neolithic settlement in many parts of Britain is patchy but the past two decades have seen a sharp rise in the discovery of Neolithic houses; in southern Sweden, Denmark, Britain and Ireland there are over 160 early Neolithic houses, many with the longest dimension of 5m and all dated to *c.*3300 cal BC or earlier (thanks to Peter Rowley-Conwy for the pre-publication information).

There are good examples of rectangular houses at Fengate in eastern England and Balleygalley in Northern Ireland, and their associations are interesting (**32**). Both have artefacts from the Langdale axe factory (**colour plate 4**) and the long-distance trade of material for axes throughout Britain has been studied in great detail by the Implement Petrology Research Group. Neolithic houses have been found in Derbyshire (Lismore Fields), Kent (White Horse Stone), Oxfordshire (Yarnton) and Perthshire (Callander).

The Fengate house was excavated in 1972 on the Padholme Road site in the Fengate area near Peterborough. The house measures 7m by 8.5m (22ft by 26ft). The walls were of wattle covered with untempered clay based on a wooden frame and the roof was probably of thatch. A corner post gave a radiocarbon date of 2445 BC, and it probably housed four to six people. In the ditches of the house a number of flint artefacts were found, but the most interesting finds were a fragment of a polished stone axe from the Langdale axe factory, Cumbria (**colour plate 4**) and a jet bead; the major source for the latter is in North Yorkshire. This is further evidence for long-distance trade, either by a series of networks or individuals travelling long distances.

More recently the excavations at Balleygalley, on the north-east coast of Northern Ireland, have revealed a house; the walls of the house would have been wooden planks laid in the slot trench with an internal double row of post-holes (**32**). This rectangular house had been deliberately abandoned and demolished and the slot trenches filled with soil. Quantities of grain have been recovered as have over 2,000 flint artefacts. There was also evidence of igneous rocks being polished for axes; the local source, Tievebulliagh, is only 32km (20 miles) away. Material from further afield was also found on the Isle of Arran and more surprisingly from the Langdale axe factory (**colour plate 4**); there are very few examples from this source in Ireland. Most Neolithic wooden houses are rectangular and relatively small, as at the site of the earliest Neolithic house in the British Isles at Ballynagilly, County Tyrone. In contrast to this type of small house (and there are many other examples in Britain) is an unusual site in Scotland at Balbridie (**33** & **34**).

This site was originally interpreted as an Anglo-Saxon hall site comparable to another one known as Doon Hill. The research design for its excavation was based on this assumption and until the first radiocarbon dates were received, which showed it was Neolithic, there was no need to alter the research design; in fact the excavation strategy did not change but it was critical that the samples for radiocarbon dating were definitely primary (i.e. not secondarily deposited). There are two ways in which this could have happened; an Anglo-Saxon house built on existing Neolithic settlement/deposits or the trees used by the Anglo-Saxons were felled in the Neolithic and survived. However, the samples were taken from the upper fills of the trenches and post-holes; they date the filling up of the features. Ten dates ranging from 2790 ± 135 bc to 3080 ± 60 bc were taken on charred remains of cereals (the site produced over 720,000 grains of cereal); a Neolithic date cannot be much in doubt. The grain also contained evidence of bread wheat as a separate crop which is not common in the Neolithic; it was probably warm enough in the early third millennium to allow bread wheat to be grown. To quote the authors of the interim report, 'the plant macrofossils recovered at this middle Deeside location, within sight of the

32 *Neolithic house at Balleygalley, Northern Ireland* Courtesy of D. Simpson

33 *Cropmarks of a Neolithic house at Balbridie, Scotland.* Crown Copyright: Royal Commission on the Ancient and Historical Monuments of Scotland

34 *The excavations at Balbridie from the air* Copyright Aberdeen Archaeological Surveys. Crown Copyright Reserved

Grampian massif . . . perhaps betoken a rather more precocious stage in the agricultural colonization of the British Isles than is frequently detected in the archaeological record'. The excavators thought that Balbridie belongs more to continental European practices than other British sites, perhaps because of immigration to this east coast? The building is the widest Neolithic building in Europe and comparable to structures in the Aisne valley in France. It is also the longest building in Neolithic Britain.

A French connection also led to the discovery of a Neolithic house in Kent, during the construction of the Channel Tunnel Rail link at White Horse Stone in a dry valley on the south-side of the scarp slope of the North Downs. The house is 18m by 8m wide, defined by large posts from which radiocarbon dates provide a date range from 3940 to 3530 cal BC, or early Neolithic. The house is situated 1km from the only megaliths in south-eastern England, on the River Medway (Kit's Coty House and Little Kit's Coty House). What is also interesting about the discovery of this site is the depth below the modern surface, some 4m (**35**, **36**).

The Orkneys

Recent work on the Neolithic sites in Orkney has shown the importance of design and lay-out on Neolithic settlements. At two sites, Skara Brae and Barnhouse, settlements of stone houses have survived very well. The Orkney islands have preserved whole landscapes of prehistoric life and nowhere is the evidence for a Neolithic village better preserved.

The story of Skara Brae has been told on many occasions, and like so many Neolithic sites its end was catastrophic (**37**). In this instance it was a natural disaster, probably due to a massive storm which swamped the site in sea and sand. This natural act also allowed its preservation for 50 centuries. The site was re-discovered to the modern world in 1850 and has been subject to excavation six times; the first systematic excavation was undertaken by Professor Gordon Childe in 1927. The site was occupied for a number of generations (perhaps 20 to 25) as there is evidence of at least four building phases. Its maximum size was achieved with eight stone-built houses (all with interconnecting passages) with a population of about 50. Each house has an entrance, a rectangular hearth and stone recesses, dressers

35 *Plan of the Early Neolithic house found during excavations in advance of the Channel Tunnel Rail Link at White Horse.* Union Railways (South) Limited

36 *Photo of the Early Neolithic house found during excavations in advance of the Channel Tunnel Rail Link at White Horse Stone, Kent.* Union Railways (South) Limited

and stone 'box' beds for sleeping; only one house had a window and all these features are stone built. The roof may have been supported by whale bones.

The coastal setting is a familiar prehistoric one and the excavations of the midden deposits show that the marine resources were well used, especially limpets (there is a suggestion that the limpets were used as fish-bait). Bones from wild (red deer) and domesticated animals (cow and sheep) were also discovered, including birds and fish. Burnt grain was also found; evidence that the combination of crops, cattle rearing and natural resources enabled the community to survive at Skara Brae for nearly 1,000 years (3200-2200 BC). The occupants were also skilled craftsmen making elaborately decorated tools, weapons and ornaments; there is also a suggestion that they painted themselves with red paint as small containers which contained red ochre have been found.

Another site in Orkney, recently discovered, is that of Barnhouse (**38**), a late Neolithic settlement, near the Stones of Stenness. The original village was constructed around 3200 BC and it is different from the village of Skara Brae. The largest house, no. 2 on the plan, is symmetrical on the axis of the doorway with six recesses (reminiscent of the burial chamber at Maes Howe, which is in view of Barnhouse today). The house had two large and elaborately constructed hearths centrally placed. The architecture of the house is similar to the passage

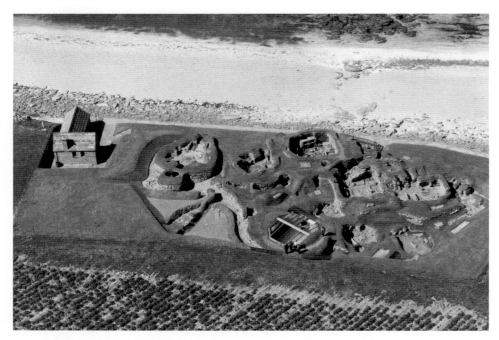

37 *Skara Brae, Orkney. A Neolithic stone-built settlement, abandoned after a storm.* Crown Copyright: Royal Commission on the Ancient and Historical Monuments of Scotland

tomb of Maes Howe and a further connection is a burial, in a stone cist (covered by a flagstone) in the south-west portion of the house. A further 15 houses were excavated and these other houses were of a different construction, being circular in shape and probably having turf roofs and comparable to many other Neolithic houses on Orkney.

The standard architecture for a Neolithic house in Orkney is the 'dresser' opposite the entrance with stone-box beds on the right and left of a stone-built hearth. As Colin Richards, the excavator at Barnhouse points out, the hearth may not have been centrally located but it did play a central role in Orcadian life; this was as true in the Neolithic as it is today. The central stone hearth has a stone-box bed to the right and left, and it has been suggested that the larger right-hand bed might have been for a male and the smaller left-hand bed for a female. Richards argues that the hearth is not just the centre of the house but the centre of the Neolithic world, the *axis mundi*, which provides an eternal reference point from which everything and everyone take their position and orientation. It provides fire and light, two essential prerequisites for life in Orkney. Keeping the fire going, and never letting it go out was an important symbol of unity and well being. The Neolithic stone hearth can be seen to have been the focal point around which the house was built.

Three further elements of the site must be noted. The circular houses were demolished and replaced whereas house 2 remained in use throughout the history of the settlement. An area to the east of house 2 in the centre of the settlement was where pottery manufacture, stone working, bone and flint working took place (in the open area between houses 6, 7, & 12). Finally the largest stone-built feature on the site, no. 8 on the plan, requires some explanation (**38**). This construction consists of an outer enclosing wall, 1.5m (4.5ft) thick and over 25m (78ft) in diameter; inside it a house-like building, with a 7m by 7m (22ft by 22ft) inner floor area with a large central hearth and a rear dresser, was encased in the 3m (10ft) thick wall. A complete grooved ware vessel was set into the floor near the eastern wall. The entrance faces north-west, the direction of the setting mid-summer sun and included a monumental porch construction. This building is the latest on the site, as it overlies earlier features and is therefore a Neolithic monument in its own right. Its exact role is open to speculation, but once again we can see the inextricable connection between domestic and ritual activity.

The Hebrides

As more and more archaeological work is done, the distribution of sites of all periods becomes wider. Excavations in Scotland and especially on North Uist (in the Outer Hebrides) have revealed a number of Neolithic settlement sites (The Udal, Eilean an Tighe, and Eilean Domhnuaill). Recent excavations at Bharpa Carinish, at the southern end of North Uist, have revealed another Neolithic house (found beneath later material). There were three stone-built hearths, five shallow pits and half a dozen small post-holes. The flint assemblage suggests domestic usage, and the macroplant assemblage contained a mix of barley, wheat, crab-apple pips, and hazelnut shells. It is difficult to convey the nature of this site as the features are ephemeral, unlike the stone walls of Barnhouse, which are eye-catching when under excavation. More often the remains of Neolithic dwellings are like those at Bharpa Carinish; maybe the stone walls which surrounded the hearths have been removed, perhaps to build a cairn nearby? This site is also like so many others in that it was discovered underneath a later more prominent monument (a long cairn). The radiocarbon dates are in the 3500 to 3000 BC range when calibrated. It is suggested that all hearths are contemporary (given they are 5,000 years old) and they were used during a 500-year period.

Wessex

In presenting this guide to Neolithic settlement, I have not deliberately ignored the usually accepted centre of prehistory – Wessex; its focal point in British prehistory is not justified in terms of settlement evidence. The superb monuments which do survive (Stonehenge, Windmill Hill, Avebury and Silbury Hill) are part of a settlement pattern in that the communities which

38 *Plan of the Neolithic settlement at Barnhouse, Orkney*

built them must have been living nearby. Research work by Bob Smith has attempted to model the settlement pattern in the Avebury region. In the early Neolithic the landscape around Avebury would have been heavily wooded and although there were clearances these were not necessarily for growing crops. The woodlands were being managed for pannage (pasture for pigs), browsing for other animals and raw materials. As time went on the woodland was further opened up in the valley corridor for pastoral and arable use. There is a suggestion that new areas were needed because weed infestation, especially by bracken, had become so rampant that it was easier to open up new areas for agricultural use than it was to manage the already cleared areas. The late Neolithic was a time of dramatic social change, suggested by large amounts of monument building going on in the area (Silbury Hill and Avebury). The faunal record suggests an increase in the use of pigs as they are a readily renewable source of fat and protein and would have been well adapted to the local environment.

The use of the valley floor for the settlements as well as agriculture is one of the reasons finding settlements sites has been so difficult. It is this low-lying environment which has been subject to deposition and alluviation. The sites may be there, but they are difficult to find. Recently Alasdair Whittle (of Cardiff University) has been excavating large curvilinear palisade enclosures in the Kennet valley, in sight of Silbury Hill. In the title of his book, *Sacred Mound Holy Rings*, Whittle is referring to the late Neolithic palisade enclosures, constructed with large oak posts. He concludes that these enclosures could have had defensive, domestic, ceremonial or sacred roles, and that these roles are not mutually exclusive. The low-lying position of the enclosures suggests defence was not paramount but the large oak posts were a symbol of power for the community, perhaps controlling the sacred mound (Silbury Hill) as well as the other monuments (long barrows and avenues) in the area. The significance of these enclosures in the British Isles is that there are fewer than ten in the whole country.

Summary

The lack of evidence for Neolithic settlement has caused many models to be proposed and new theories expounded. The evidence for farming in the Neolithic period in England was mainly based on extrapolation from Europe, where there were many longhouses, especially from the Linerbankeramik sites in central Europe. When some of the sites (in Scandinavia especially) were excavated and revealed to be burials or similar to causewayed enclosures, questions were raised about the basis of the evidence for farming in Britain. This was also the time when new approaches to examining sites in the landscape were being proposed and it was conceivable that the first major monuments (long barrows, bank barrow and causewayed enclosures) were the product of a mobile (but wealthy) society and not the product of farming communities. Thus, it was the fashion to suggest that there was no *permanent settlement* in the Neolithic; the pit scatters, flint working areas could be seen as the major evidence for short-lived campsites; the population living on wild foodstuffs in a nomadic society. This model was based on a lack of evidence but the excavation of a number of key sites showed that in the early Neolithic there were substantial houses, built from massive timber posts, with internal wooden divisions; the houses at Balbridie and Callander were built in this way. However, it was not only the size and construction of the houses but the environmental remains which provide the evidence for a re-interpretation of

Neolithic farming in Britain. Peter Rowley-Conwy and Coinneach Maclean, as well as Alan Fairweather have examined thousands of cereal remains from Balbridie and agree on their identification as emmer wheat, naked barley and bread wheat. Rowley-Conwy in particular contests the view there was little farming in the Neolithic and that the house at Balbridie was an unoccupied store and a ceremonial focus for nomadic groups. The evidence points much more to the cultivation of crops and some permanent settlements. The increase in the number of houses found in Britain (and now Europe; four Neolithic houses were found in Denmark in 1997 alone) also indicates the fact that there were settled aspects of the Neolithic in Britain. The house at White Horse Stone in Kent, buried 4m deep under colluvium, is strong evidence that much more evidence for Neolithic houses lies buried and awaits discovery. The material from Scotland is equally persuasive for Neolithic 'village settlements'.

Our perceptions of what life was like in the Neolithic and the settlements have changed dramatically in under a century. The discoveries of Skara Brae and Barnhouse and the associated monumental architecture show that socially, economically, and technologically the communities were highly skilled. In the following quotation taken from a Rudyard Kipling 'Just So Story' published at the turn of the century, the view once held of Neolithic man as a cave-dwelling savage is now seen as antiquated.

> Once upon a most early time was a Neolithic man. He was not a Jute, or even a Dravidian, which he might well have been, Best Beloved, but never mind why. He was a Primitive, and he lived cavily in a Cave, and he wore very few clothes, and he couldn't read and he couldn't write and he didn't want to, except when he was hungry he was quite happy.

> Rudyard Kipling
> *Just So Stories*, 1902

5

BRONZE AGE SETTLEMENT

The past 20 years have seen a dramatic increase in our knowledge and understanding of how people lived in the Bronze Age. We know a great deal about the burial practices; antiquarians opened up thousands of barrows as a leisurely pursuit in the nineteenth and early twentieth centuries. The ubiquity of Bronze Age burials throughout Britain has allowed for the predominance of the study of death for this period to continue. This is exemplified by Fox's *Life and Death in the Bronze Age*, published in 1959; in the preface the author admits that the book is about Bronze Age barrow excavation!

So, was the Bronze Age any different from the Neolithic? There was a change in the landscape during the late third and early second millennium. Settlements which might be described as permanent begin to be developed and the landscape is controlled to a much greater degree. Linear boundaries are a feature of the Bronze Age throughout England, especially in Wessex, Dartmoor, and Yorkshire.

The technological change, from stone to bronze, did not happen overnight and there is good archaeological evidence for a considerable overlap. The use of bronze in Europe was normally preceded by copper artefacts, but in Britain the Copper Age is virtually non-existent. If the Bronze Age is not just about death and burial it can be linked with metalwork typologies. Significant and abundant amounts of Bronze Age metalwork (gold as well as bronze) have been discovered and analysed in terms of typology and date. Recent research is focusing on the context of the metalwork (as much has been found on settlements) rather than its typology. However, the Bronze Age is ushered in by changes in pottery style with the arrival of a new form: beakers; finely-made, tall, and elaborately decorated pottery.

The Beaker phenomenon

Whole books have been written on the Beaker folk (2700-1700 BC) and there has been much discussion in the archaeological literature about the nature of the beakers themselves and the supposed 'folk' who used them. Were they immigrants who brought in a new bronze-working technology and beakers? Or did the use of these fashionable objects spread as fashions do, by personal recommendation, trade and simple copying? Nobody admits to knowing the answer and the spread of Beakers must have been a combination of movement of peoples as well as the diffusion of ideas beyond the areas where the originators moved; their distribution spreads from Algeria in the south to Norway in the north, Britain in the west and the Danube in the east. Diffusion, as a factor in understanding change, has been unfashionable in modern archaeology, having been popular 40 years ago, but with all trends and fashions (especially modern fashions of thinking) it is important to hang on to the better parts of past interpretations and not discard them altogether. Diffusion falls into this category and the ways in which ideas and ultimately objects move around and are copied should be part of the study of diffusion in prehistory. As mentioned in the previous chapter, recent social and political events in Europe and the Middle East have led to a greater understanding of the importance of the movement of people and not just their artefacts and ideas.

The recurring theme of death and burial is nowhere better exemplified than in the Beaker period; a classic Beaker burial would have contained a 'package' of (Beaker) arrowheads, wristguards and daggers. The recent discovery of the archer's burial in Amesbury, Wiltshire not only reinforces the point that, for the Beaker period, it is the burials which provide the most information but also the distances some of the objects have moved; some of the metalwork appears to have come from central Europe at a very early date. The question of where these people lived has usually been answered from negative evidence; we cannot find the sites so they must have lived in temporary settlements which could be easily moved. However, the truth is that we do not know what the settlement system was. Even quite sophisticated tented settlements can be moved in a matter of hours; any society which had such organised burial practices is likely to have a similarly sophisticated settlement organisation. There are two reasons why finding Beaker settlements is difficult; one is that current archaeological techniques are not sufficient to locate Beaker settlements and the other is that post-depositional factors are such that these sites may have been lost or obscured. There is no doubt that this is a period of change, even invasion and migration into the British Isles from Europe.

Belle Tout

There is, of course, always one exception and that is a cliff-top site on the south coast of England at Belle Tout (**39**). The site is situated on virgin chalk downland with cliffs rising up 84m (255ft) from the sea, only 3km (1.9 miles) west of Beachy Head. The Beaker settlement is situated in an area of high archaeological activity with round barrows and an Iron Age promontory fort nearby. The site itself comprises overlapping rectangular earthwork enclosures which have been truncated by the cliff-edge (a process which has been going

39 *Belle Tout, Beaker settlement where there are three sorts of house; a wide oval, built with continuous construction trench (4); a rectilinear house built with post holes (5), and an oval one built with post holes (6)*

for many years, at a rate of 2m (6ft) per year). The site was first discovered in 1909 and the erosion was evident then.

The excavator, Richard Bradley, suggests the site was continuously occupied (and not seasonally, as is often suggested for late Neolithic and early Bronze Age sites); this is based on the fact that the pottery is local and there appear to be permanent structures. Cattle herding was probably important – the enclosures and other associated ditches are interpreted as stock enclosures. The large amount of flint scrapers discovered suggests the preparation of hides was an important activity at the site.

The Beaker period is often seen as the transition from the Neolithic to the Bronze Age, although the use of metal was prevalent before the Beakers themselves arrived. The extent to which Beaker-type artefacts were adopted or the Beaker folk invaded is still an unresolved matter, and as with most complex questions there is no simple, or single answer. From a settlement point of view there is no distinctive Beaker settlement type. The second half of the third millennium and the second millennium are characterised by the dividing up of the landscape, not just into settlements but with extensive linear boundaries and field systems.

Dividing up the land

Landscapes with settlements as hamlets, clusters of houses, fields systems and linear earthworks, sometimes associated with settlements, are characteristic of Bronze Age land use. Organising the land into areas for ranching was an important activity at this time in prehistory.

It is different from the Neolithic in that extensive areas have been 'organised', even controlled, and the remains of this control have survived. These extensive Bronze Age landscapes have been discovered using techniques of aerial and terrestrial survey which developed quickly after 1945. These landscapes are not yet fully understood but a number, particularly in the south-west and north-east of England, have been well recorded. Between 1970 and 1980 two approaches to archaeological work were expanding. One was for preservation and the other for excavation. Preservation strategies rely on detailed surveys and more investigative survey is being done in Britain now than ever before, as the following examples show. Some of these are based on projects which form part of English Heritage's National Mapping Programme (NMP).

Bodmin Moor, Cornwall

Bodmin Moor is one of the best preserved and accessible areas of prehistoric settlement in Britain. The following case-study, based on the work supplied by Nick Johnson, the County Archaeologist for Cornwall, concentrates on a small area 2km by 3km (1.25 by 1.8 miles) and develops from what was 'known' in the last century, a few settlements, cairns, stone circles, and areas of peat bogs depicted on First Edition Ordnance Survey (OS) maps, which were published in 1891.

The aerial photograph (**colour plate 5**) shows a stone-built hillfort, which although not on the early maps had been recorded; it may have Neolithic origins but is generally assumed to be Bronze Age. The 1976 OS revised map for the area shows this additional information, a series of settlements, linear boundaries and cairns. Much of the 'known' area was protected by legislation (as scheduled ancient monuments), but unless our surveys are comprehensive and thorough, areas and sites cannot be protected.

In 1980 an air survey plot was completed by the former RCHME and material was added from this survey (**40, 41**). This emphasises the value, and the necessity, of using as many survey techniques as possible; the aerial survey involved both the taking of aerial photographs and mapping from them. This work was then followed by survey in the field, undertaken by the Cornwall Archaeological Unit. These surveys demonstrate that it is not just a matter of adding new material but also understanding the landscape. Limited information about the stratigraphic relationship can be obtained from aerial photography so questions about which features are earlier or later than others

Roughtor, N

a

Roughtor

Fernacre

Roughtor, S

b

Stannon Down

Louden

c

Garrow

d

Stannon, S

0   1000 m

0   1000 yd

○ Small simple cairn	◖ Long cairn	⦂⦂⦂ Stone circle
⊖ Small simple cairn with cist	⊙ Tor cairn	•••• Stone row
▫ Small kerbed cairn	⣿ Clearance cairns	ᨊᨊᨊ Stone setting
▪ Small kerbed cairn with cist	○ Large simple cairn	⊥ Standing stone
△ Platform cairn	☐ Large kerbed cairn	• Hut
▲ Rimmed platform cairn	■ Large kerbed cairn with cist	▨ Bog and stream
◆ Rimmed platform cairn with kerb(s)		

40 *Extract from the Bodmin Moor survey plan using air and ground survey techniques. The remains depicted here are probably from the Bronze Age c.1900 BC to 1000 BC.* Crown Copyright, NMR

41 *Aerial photograph of Bodmin Moor showing settlements and fields.* Crown Copyright. NMR, SX 1480/30/286

can only be answered by analytical field survey (and ultimately small-scale excavation).

In analysing the landscape figure **40** shows at 'a' that the curvilinear field system is overlain by major field boundary. This feature was only understood after fieldwork in 1985 and not by the previous ground surveys or the air survey.

At 'b' the settlement is overlain by a D-shaped enclosure with linear boundary attached which runs into the bog (**40**). The relationship of the D-shaped enclosure to the underlying settlement is obviously an important one. It was interpreted through field survey to overly the settlement. The same survey approach for 'c' showed that the settlement and parts of field system were overlain by major field boundary. Similarly at 'd' the re-use of an earlier field system created a major field boundary which runs into a bog at the south-eastern end; more work is recommended in this area.

The purpose of going into some detail is to show the way in which archaeological surveyors think and work. The next stage is to understand and present the interpretations. Having done this analysis the chronology for the different settlements could be suggested. All fall within the Bronze Age but could be divided into time bands.

On figure **40** three different phases are represented with three Bronze Age dates: 1900, 1500, and 1000 BC or later. Those areas which have not been closely dated are still Bronze Age but could be anywhere in the second millennium BC. Although the majority of the stone-built features are settlements, there a few ritual monuments associated with these settlements.

Having understood in some detail one of the highest concentrations of Bronze Age archaeology there has to be a strategy for conserving the landscape. To this end the Cornwall Unit made proposals to English Heritage and many of the sites on Bodmin Moor have now been protected. As part of a nationwide Monuments Protection Programme all sites and landscapes are being re-assessed with a view to greater protection. On other parts of Bodmin Moor there are other equally well-preserved sites which require further investigation, field survey and excavation as an aid to management and understanding, notably Stowe's Pound (**colour plate 9**). Recent re-examination at Leskernick (**42**) has confirmed the Bronze Age date but also examined the landscape setting of the two settlements there (a western and southern one) comprising 51 circular stone houses, and the significance of rocks and stones in the landscape. Each house was visited by the archaeological team and a mock wooden door-frame used to attempt to see what the width of the view would have been and the possible implications this may have had on the occupants; the interim report of the first season is well worth reading (see Bender *et al. Proceedings of the Prehistoric Society* for 1997).

Dartmoor

In contrast to the above part of Bodmin Moor with its settlements, there is another moorland landscape, Dartmoor, which has a network of field systems,

42 *Leskernick, Bodmin Moor, Cornwall. A stone-built Bronze Age settlement built over a long period with new circular houses and fields being added as the settlement grew.* Crown Copyright NMR

Centred at SX 18287999

Boulder, stone walls (no apparent structural form)

Upright curb slabs

Cairns

Clitter spread (sketch graded according to density)

Natural boulders (surveyed)

Slopes

Disused Leat

known as reaves, and their associated settlements (**43** & **44**). Although similar in date to Bodmin the contrast in land-use pattern is interesting. These reaves were originally thought to be a mixture of prehistoric (small fields) and medieval (long fields). This story is one which Andrew Fleming has described as 'a curious case of lost knowledge'. One question he raises is why, when the reaves were published in the *Proceedings of the Prehistoric Society* in 1952 (not even an obscure county journal), did it take so long for their place in prehistory to be realised? The answer is partly fashion, and partly having the right people in the right place with 'open minds'.

The reaves date from 1700-1600 BC and were in use for approximately 600-700 years. They were laid out in an open landscape and pollen analysis has confirmed this. The word reave is from Old English *raew* meaning a row, whether stones, houses or walls. On Dartmoor the name reave is given to any low bank or line of stones, whatever its purpose.

The whole system of fields which criss-cross the Dartmoor landscape have had different names applied to them, aggregate or cohesive, but Fleming has coined the phrase 'coaxial' for this type of system which is laid out systematically on one major axis. Since the term was coined, coaxial systems have been found in the west of Ireland (Behy-Glenurla and on the Burren), on Bodmin Moor, in northern England in Swaledale, at Grassington and on the South Yorkshire/Nottinghamshire border, in Lincolnshire at Goltho, at Fengate near Peterborough, in Norfolk and Suffolk and across southern England from Cornwall (West Penwith) through Dorset and Wessex, including the Lambourn Downs to Black Patch in Sussex. This is only the tip of the iceberg and as more survey work (using aerial survey and field survey) is being done, more of these field systems are being discovered, partly through English Heritage's National Mapping Programme.

Figure **43** is a plan of the Dartmeet system. The houses, 'black blobs', cluster in a neighbourly way, but are they all contemporary? This is one of the best examples of an articulated landscape; the Combestone Way (CW) runs all the way across the system at right angles to the main system (in four different stretches). Ring cairns and large cairns occur within the system and just beyond the terminal reave. A triple stone row lies just beyond the terminal reave and may have helped to determine its position. The reaves have a preference for running straight up the hillside at right angles to valley or river, except where common sense prevailed and they had to follow the contour.

The settlements and individual houses were not evenly distributed but clustered; the fields furthest away from houses are relatively large and rectilinear; near the house they are much smaller, more numerous and curvilinear. It was these small irregular fields which early scholars thought were prehistoric, the linear reaves medieval. Figure **43** shows about 40 houses on Dartmeet and about 80 fields and gives a good indication of Bronze Age houses and immediate fields. There is variability in the exact detail of the

43 *Dartmoor: part of the Dartmeet parallel reave system on Holne Moor showing houses and reaves. The black blobs (houses) appear to cluster into neighbourly groups.* After Fleming

houses and the reaves but they all are within fields. The Ripon Tor parallel system on Horridge Common shows well on an aerial photograph (**44**). Fleming refers to these clusters of houses as 'neighbourhood groups'; elsewhere, on Yar Tor, the houses are evenly distributed in fields of large size. Some of these have their domestic enclosures around them and were perhaps part of a later additional settlement especially as Yar Tor is one of the most exposed places on Dartmoor.

Transverse reaves appear to be crucial in understanding the articulation of the settlements within the wider landscape, as they define small fields near the houses, and larger fields further away. This helps to predict where settlements may have been but have been obscured or destroyed. Given this 'system' of houses and two sizes of field, what was the system of ownership? It is not easy to prove ownership on the basis of land divisions but it is unlikely that the land was not divided on inheritance. Sometimes the house pre-dates the reaves, some are contemporary and others postdate the reave system.

One major question is 'who built the system'? Was it one large organiser who owned it like an estate, or a collective action? Fleming argues for an aggregate of smaller units (neighbourhood groups) in which the community was important, if not essential, to its survival and not very different from many rural areas around the world today. A comparative Welsh example is the *trefgordd*, which Fleming describes as 'a working unit of co-operative dairy farming . . . the natural group of homesteads of relatives or neighbours acting

44 *Dartmor: Ripon Tor on Horridge Common, showing the parallel reaves, which are closer together near the houses and more widely spaced away from the houses.* Crown Copyright NMR, SX 7574/23

together as a single community as regards their cattle and their ploughing'. Legally the *trefgordd* was defined as 'nine houses and one plough and one oven, and one churn and one cock and one bull and one herdsman'. The size of the neighbourhood group can only be guessed at but it was big enough to be able to operate in an organised manner, perhaps in the region of 25. It is unlikely that there were individual farms as the domestic enclosure could not feed a family. Also, there is variability of the lay-out of houses and enclosures but not all elements of a farm are exhibited and were perhaps shared amongst a community. The land was farmed by a group, not individuals. There are few lanes and droveways which suggests there was no concept of ownership and so, perhaps, there was no need for separate lanes.

There are, however, other settlements on Dartmoor which are presumed to be Bronze Age but are different (and impressive) in that they appear to be villages (**45**). Fleming sees these sites as local centres.

Dartmoor is a prehistoric landscape often viewed as marginal land; marginal in terms of agricultural production as well as marginal to the centres of population of modern Britain. It is more famous for its prison and Jamaica Inn than for its archaeology. In the Bronze Age there is evidence to suggest that Dartmoor may have been a central place, not just for settlement but also for the spiritual and ritual side of life. This recalls us to the theme of not being able to separate the domestic and functional from the religious and ritual. There are five stone circles on North Moor, which are regularly spaced and may well be contemporary, and therefore could be a ceremonial centre for the area. This reinforces the idea that Dartmoor was central to the Bronze Age communities in the area.

It is worth mentioning a methodological point which highlights the difference between the Bodmin and Dartmoor surveys. Fleming measured in

45 *Rider's Ring, a Bronze Age settlement on Dartmoor.* Crown Copyright NMR, SX 6764/15

the reaves by setting up base lines by eye and off-setting; he then used an 'EDM' (electronic distance measuring system) for accurate recording of all features. In *Dartmoor Reaves* he says, 'In landscape archaeology there is always something new to notice. Given the right level of organisation and resources, we would perhaps have plotted the Dartmeet system from air photos and field checked it in a couple of seasons. If we had done it this way, our checking would have been essentially working outwards from a piece of paper, our provisional plot; the method which we actually developed, though slower, was much more responsive to what was actually on the ground.' This is a fair point but there is an interpretation stage of working with aerial photographs, and the production of that provisional plot is enormously cost-effective especially if it is the same people who are doing the aerial photographic interpretation and the field checking. As both these examples show, there is much to be gained from using all the techniques available to us.

Before leaving Dartmoor there is another area, Shaugh Moor, which has added to our understanding of the landscape and individual settlements of the Bronze Age. Traditionally it was thought that the Dartmoor area would have been visited by prehistoric people who travelled some distance to use the moor as summer pasture. Excavations at an enclosure on Dean Moor, which contained 11 stone-based buildings, demonstrated that it was more than a summer sheepfold. There was evidence for a number of activities including spinning, pottery manufacture, corn grinding, and even cheese making. Whetstones were found in every house which suggested that bronze tools were sharpened for regular use.

More recent excavations by Geoffrey Wainwright at another enclosure, Shaugh Moor enclosure 15 (**46**), also provided evidence for a number of activities. This circular enclosure had no discernible entrance (except for what was perhaps a stile) and contained five stone-built circular houses (**46**). Each house contained a saddle-quern and all but one house a whetstone. The theme introduced earlier of every site being open to re-interpretation arises here; initially the site was interpreted as having been occasionally visited by small groups of people for the trade of metal and agricultural produce. This practice could have gone on for over 1,000 years based on radiocarbon dates (1600 to 600 BC). An alternative view is that the houses were built sometime around 1700-1600 BC and the enclosure wall soon afterwards. A couple of hundred years later the buildings were refurbished and projecting stone porches added. Most of the occupation took place within the space of 400 years and the enclosure was visited only occasionally after that, but especially around 600 BC.

Before leaving the south-west there is a recently excavated site at Trethellan farm, near Newquay, which is a good example of a lowland Bronze Age settlement with seven houses and associated 'ritual' structures. The houses were situated on a level terrace with associated fields, where there is evidence for arable cultivation. House 2222 at Trethellan farm provides a good example of the Bronze Age round house which was common throughout Britain at the time. An interesting aspect of Trethellan farm is the continuity of use at the site; after the Bronze Age settlement had been abandoned the site was not used for nearly 900 years. As the excavator, Jacqui Nowakowski, explains, there is good evidence for continuity of settlement from the Bronze Age to the Iron Age. At this site the continuity was not in terms of settlement; the Iron Age

46 *Shaugh Moor Enclosure 15, Dartmoor under excavation.* Crown Copyright. Photo courtesy of City of Plymouth Museum and Art Gallery

47 *Reconstruction of the Bronze Age settlement on Itford Hill, Sussex.* After P. Burke

community used the area as a cemetery. It is possible that the remains of the house were still visible 900 years after having been abandoned and that this gave the area a special significance, which was interpreted as in some way spiritual by the Iron Age communities.

Southern England

The theme of the round house can be continued if we move to the chalk downlands of southern England. There are two sites which summarise the state of knowledge for the Bronze Age settlement on the chalk in southern England. The first is Itford Hill, a farmstead (**47**) surrounded by fields. It was a mixed farming settlement raising crops of barley and other cereals and stock raising with sheep and oxen. Probably only one family lived here for economic and social reasons. There is some evidence of ritual activity – a chalk phallus was discovered and it perhaps represents some sort of fertility cult. The main settlement appears to have been planned and built as a complete farmstead with two sleeping huts, a weaving hut and storage hut, a cooking compound, and eight other huts serving as store rooms, barns, byres and workshops. There were perhaps 20 people living here for over 25 years. The radiocarbon dates give a range of 1000–750 BC. There is no evidence as to why the site was abandoned. In the excavation report 13 other similar sites in similar locations on the Downs are referred to; only one of these – Black Patch – has been excavated.

In 1979 Peter Drewett was able to say that the site of Itford Hill, Sussex (**47**), although excavated over 40 years ago, is still one of our main sources for the function of Middle Bronze Age round houses. More work on similar sites was necessary to confirm and expand on the initial interpretations; one site which was excavated was Black Patch also in Sussex, only 5km (3.1 miles) east of Itford Hill. The dating of the sites through radiocarbon gives them a date of 1000 bc.

At Black Patch five certain structures were excavated and each structure was on a house platform or terrace, made level from the chalk slopes. The size of the houses was always a matter for discussion and until re-interpretations in the 1970s and finally, the excavations at Black Patch (**48**), the size and construction of these houses could be suggested. They are similar in size to the later Iron Age round houses; initially the post-holes which supported the inner ring of posts was thought to be the full extent of the houses. The excavations at Black Patch revealed large areas of flint nodules which are interpreted as having been the base for the walls. The charcoal from the site was mainly from oak (with some hazel and hawthorn) and oak would have provided superb material for the post and rafters, while the other types of wood were used for making wattle walls and a framework for thatch.

Drewett's excavations also broke new ground in recording in detail the position of all artefacts and ecofacts within the huts. Two huts of exactly similar size, shape and construction had different functions; the evidence was derived from this detailed recording and approach and was summarised diagrammatically (**48**, **49**, **50**). From this the social organisation of a Bronze Age community has been inferred with Hut 3 (**49**) being the chief's hut (or the Head's hut according to the excavator). The whole compound is thought to contain no more than a single conjugal family (assuming a society in which individuals had one partner each), perhaps one family with adult, unmarried siblings. The interpretation as offered in figure **50** is very much a reflection of our own society where it is assumed that food preparation is women's work and that because razors were found in Hut 3 this is a man's hut. This may in fact be correct but we must be wary of imposing our own values on people 3,000 years ago. Did women shave in the Bronze Age? Did men prepare the food at Black Patch? Is there any reason why the Head of the group was a man? (**49**, **50**)

Understanding settlements and houses

Circularity is a feature of settlements within the Neolithic and right up to Roman times, but it is not exclusive as there are many rectilinear structures, be they houses, settlements or burials. In the Bronze Age and later the main design is the round-house. Apart from the ease of design and construction there is no defining reason for this shape, and on the continent there are many rectangular houses. The organisation of space and the location of the doorway can tell us much about these houses; the majority have entrances to the east, perhaps evoking a cosmological metaphor for the house and the universe, and an easterly

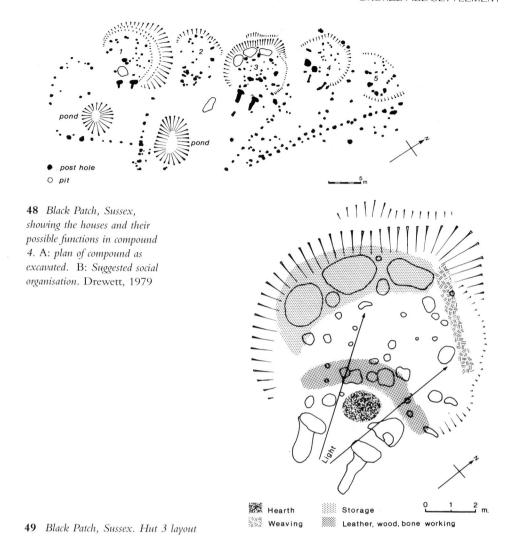

● post hole
○ pit

5 m

48 *Black Patch, Sussex, showing the houses and their possible functions in compound 4. A: plan of compound as excavated. B: Suggested social organisation. Drewett, 1979*

Light

▨ Hearth   ▦ Storage
▧ Weaving   ▒ Leather, wood, bone working

0 1 2 m.

49 *Black Patch, Sussex. Hut 3 layout*

sunrise (or it was simply to avoid the prevailing wind?). Any arrangement of space will involve discussions of left/right, light/dark, upper/lower, birth/death and good/evil. We can never know exactly what the reasons for the patterning of debris within houses was but there is plenty of room for speculation and a vast literature containing anthropological theories from Lévi-Strauss, Bourdieu, Hodder and Tambiah and many others. The key to gaining some understanding is to assess the evidence from archaeology and explore the many options for its interpretation; there may be no right or wrong answer but the exploration of possibilities will shed light on the wide range of possibilities for human action.

A number of researchers have commented on the paucity of material left behind; this indicates that regular clearing out of the house was essential and the

50 *Black Patch, Sussex. Reconstruction of activities inside the house*

discovery of very large midden sites (for example at Potterne and Chisenbury) may be the clue for this. The land-fill sites of today have their forebears but we have yet to discover them in the numbers they must have existed.

New approaches to understanding the dynamics of Middle and Late Bronze Age settlement have been postulated by one researcher, Joanna Brück. She maintains that there are metaphorical connections between people, houses, pots and quernstones in Bronze Age settlements. The argument runs that if these objects were viewed as living entities then they would be treated as almost human, and reflected in the way in which the house was used. At Trethellan Farm the houses were buried at the end of their life, deliberately sealed and levelled, and at Penhale Moor, also in Cornwall the house was 'killed', if that is what the spearhead driven through the floor was meant to indicate. Just as the human population was re-born each generation, so the houses were recreated at Trethellan on the same site as the previous houses.

The metaphorical concept is also pre-eminent in the interpretations of a Late Bronze Age and Early Iron Age site at Cladh Hallan, on South Uist, in the Western Isles of Scotland (**52**). In this instance it is the connection between the use of space and the deposition of burials and artefacts within houses which is seen to fit the *sunwise model* (first suggested for the Iron Age in Wessex). This model sees the use of space within a house reflecting the passage of the sun from sunrise, in the east for living and eating (also a metaphor for birth) and sunset in the west (through to the north-east), as the sleeping, darkest quarter (reflecting death). Although this model was developed for the much larger Iron Age houses, especially Dunston Park, Berkshire, it has been used to help interpret Bronze Age dwellings in Scotland. At Cladh Hallan, where the excavations are being run by a team from Sheffield University led by Mike Parker Pearson, a series of houses has been discovered; a row of three being described as terraced housing, presumably the first in Scotland (**52**). In total six houses have been excavated and excellent preservation of a total of sixteen floor layers has provided remarkable information about the everyday life of the occupants. There is a good basis for interpretations, based on the sunwise model for the burials found. Four individuals were found beneath the floors in three houses; aside from anything else, these are thought to have been 'foundation events', made before the house was erected. All the burials were in the north-east quarter of the houses. In the southern house there was the burial of a 3-year-old child, a 12-year-old child in the central and an adult male (aged between 35 and 39) in the northern house; the fourth burial, an adult female aged between 45 and 60, was buried beneath the floor of the northern house, in the southern quadrant. All the burials were beneath later floors and had pits and post-holes cut into them, reinforcing the concept that they were deposited in a foundation ritual.

The central house, the most imposing and possible high status dwelling, had a layer in the entrance area which contained a scattered deposit of clay mould fragments for making bronze swords, spears and other armaments, together with crucible fragments. Although the evidence is not strong the most likely

51 *Black Patch, Sussex. Reconstruction of compound 4 showing house and fields.* Drewett 1982, drawn by Lysbeth Drewett

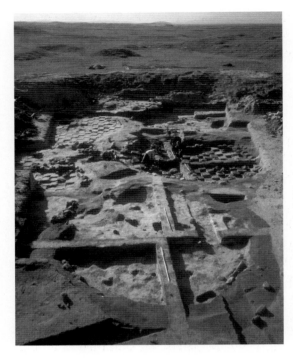

52 *Cladh Hallan, South Uist, Scotland. A Late Bronze Age settlement with substantial houses.* Copyright M. Parker Pearson

metalworking area is to the rear of the settlement. However, the significance of this bronze metalwork is that it represents long-distance connections, which is new for the Late Bronze Age in the Western Isles, but more common further south on Skye and the mainland, so not totally unexpected. The long-distance connections are reinforced by the discovery of a penannular gold-plated bronze ring (known as hair or money rings) found outside the northern house. This is the first on these islands but they are common in Ireland and other parts of the British Isles, usually in a burial context; this the only one from a settlement site in Britain.

It has always been my view that although there may be many outward manifestations of changes in our everyday life in the twenty-first century AD, when compared to prehistory there are still many fundamental similarities in the basic needs and aspirations, be it the need for food, shelter and comfort.

Pioneering analysis of protein residues from inside some of the pots show these to be cow's milk, perhaps indicating cooking of an early form of porridge (using barley rather than oats)? This scientific breakthrough also indicates that dairy cows were a common phenomenon at the site and thus there was a stable and sustainable food supply.

Cladh Hallan has a trivial but sharp reminder of our closeness with the past: the discovery in an abandoned fourth house, adjacent to the southern house, of a dump of canine faeces amongst which was found a bone blade, perhaps the world's first 'pooper scooper'; two dog skeletons were found under the floor of the central house, which the excavator suggests was part of a sacrificial event. (As this excavation is still ongoing the best source for information is the website: www.shef.ac.uk/~ap/research/hebrides/hallan.)

River gravels

Having so far concentrated on upland sites, there is a wealth of information contained in the gravels of Britain which deserves attention. As explained in the early chapters, cropmarks are a common phenomenon throughout the British Isles, but the soils above river gravels produce good cropmarks, as they are usually free draining. This biases our understanding of these areas as we are seeing only those sites which form cropmarks; other sites, buried by alluvium, remain hidden until excavated. Recent work has shown that there is just as much to be gained (if not more) from excavating in the river floodplains where cropmarks have not formed as there is from excavating cropmark sites. That said, the information which we can obtain from cropmark sites is good.

The Thames Valley is famous for its cropmarks and a survey, using aerial photographs alone, completed in the 1990s (as part of the National Mapping Programme) recorded 908 Bronze Age sites. The majority were round barrows (866) but a small number were identified as 'enclosures' and associated ditches (c.19 in all) which provides the basis for further research. The work of *Oxford Archaeology* has done much to help us understand the Thames Valley and its sites and landscape. One of the areas researched from aerial photography and excavation is the area around Reading. Here the question of the abandonment of late Bronze Age settlements in one small area of the Thames valley, the junction of Kennet and Thames, highlights the way we can understand the changing settlement pattern in prehistory. There are eight excavated sites, c.0.5km to 1.5km (0.3-1 mile) apart in the space of 6km, all near a high-status site, Marshall's Hill. Most of the sites are likely to have been pastoral settlements (perhaps having some cereal production). The point of interest here is the importance of the confluence of the two rivers (Kennet and Thames), where we have good evidence for settlement (**53**) as well as an area of the densest concentrations of riverine finds of prestige metal-work in the Thames valley. Throwing your best sword, palstave or axe into the river (or whatever expanse of water was near) was an important Bronze Age ritual; linking the settlements with this ritual activity helps us understand more about the Bronze Age way of life, and the importance of natural water supply.

In the twentieth century we tend to forget how important rivers and a consistent water supply are in everyday life. To a society dependent on a natural supply of water for drinking and daily use, as well as for longer

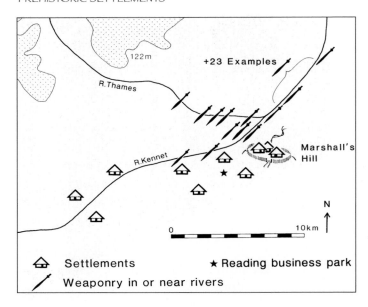

122m

+23 Examples

R.Thames

R.Kennet

Marshall's
Hill

N

0   10km

★ Reading business park

⌂ Settlements

◢ Weaponry in or near rivers

53 *Location of settlements and deposits of weaponry at the confluence of the Thames and Kennet rivers.* Copyright Oxford Archaeological Unit

distance communications, propitiation to the *gods of water* can only be expected, if this is what the discarded bronze artefacts represent. Disposal of wealth also maintained the value of the objects. The high-status site of Marshall's Hill is also strategic, overlooking the Kennet valley and confluence of the Thames and Kennet, as well as controlling route ways through the Goring Gap. It has been argued that high-status sites depended for their existence on a prestige-goods economy and that the collapse of that economy may be the reason for the abandonment of settlement in this area. Other areas of the Thames valley throughout the Bronze Age may have invested in large cattle herds (which may have inhibited agricultural expansion) and there is an increasing amount of evidence for major land boundaries in the Upper Thames Valley (around Lechlade, for example) which may have been required for the control of stock.

Although the Thames Valley is a single river valley there is a huge diversity in its archaeology. In the lower part of the valley there is a well-known site at Mucking; this is not unique as a settlement, except that it has been excavated. The prehistoric site might be described as a mini-hillfort of late Bronze Age date (**54**). The two concentric circles, which form a defended settlement, guarded the Mucking creek and ridge routeway in the ninth century BC; another nearby site formed a similar function. The linear features visible in the photograph date from the earlier Bronze Age and the later Romano-British period (there is also a villa nearby). The smaller circular features are Iron Age huts and the even smaller splodges are Saxon huts which contained sunken floors. Being on the gravel terraces this area was good for settlement from the Mesolithic through to the post-Roman

54 *Aerial photograph of the crop marks at Mucking, Essex. The concentric double ring is a Late Bronze Age 'mini-hillfort'. The rectangular outlines are of fields of Romano-British date, overlying earlier prehistoric fields.*
Cambridge University Collection of Air Photographs: copyright reserved

period; after that it would have been prime agricultural land. Therein lies the seeds of its own destruction as the plough flattened it. This enabled archaeologists to re-discover it, only for the gravel companies to obliterate the site. Excavations in the 1970s and 1980s have at least recorded the site.

Northern Britain

So far I have concentrated on southern landscapes; upland, gravel and chalk. This is deliberate as they have been under the most threat from agricultural intensification (ploughing), industrial developments and urban expansion and they have been intensively surveyed. There are other areas where the preservation is equally good, or better, and for which we have evidence for settlement from the Bronze Age.

The first is the chalk area of the Yorkshire Wolds of east Yorkshire which has been surveyed and interpreted from the air and mapped using thousands of aerial photographs as part of what is now English Heritage's National Mapping Programme (see Cathy Stoertz's *Ancient Landscapes of the Yorkshire Wolds*). This publication has analysed the information on thousands of aerial photographs taken over fifty years, and yet since its publication new discoveries are still being made. Thus, we must always re-visit previous conclusions but the summary maps for the Wolds show the remarkable way in which the land was divided up in the Bronze Age, and the intensity of use since the Neolithic to the present day (**55**). It is more than a sad irony that the reason we are able to record these landscapes in such detail is because they are visible as cropmarks in fields of wheat and

95

Later prehistoric defended sites

Defended sites and linear features

● Excavated sites
● Possible defended sites
○ Other large curvilinear features

55 *A group of curvilinear defended enclosures on the Yorkshire Wolds, derived from an aerial photographic survey (see Stoertz 1997 in further reading).* Crown Copyright, NMR

barley. In fact we are witnessing the gradual but irreversible destruction of the sites, which have been preserved in the soil for over 4,000 years. Not only are the sites being eroded but also the soil is being blown away or is moving downslope. Soon there will be no soil at all on the upper chalk slopes.

Non-survey work in the area has focused on a site called Paddock Hill, Thwing (**56**, **57**) (comparable in terms of form with the double ring at Mucking); the site was initially thought to be a henge monument but excavation soon showed it to be a Bronze Age ringwork (defended) settlement which continued in use (intermittently) until the Anglo-Saxon period. Apart from the importance of this site, as it has been excavated, it is only one of many other sites in this area of similar form. More significant, though, is the fact that the linear features which are visible on the aerial photographs are contemporary and form part of a large network of linear banks and ditches which continue for many miles across this chalk landscape (**56**). There are now many examples of this dividing up of the landscape, especially on the chalk downlands of England. The Yorkshire Wolds can be referred to as the Wessex of the North and it remains an important area for new archaeological discoveries.

As I have already mentioned there is more survey work being undertaken in Britain than has been done previously; landscapes and sites are being recorded as never before. Recent work by the former RCHME in the Yorkshire Dales (**58**) has highlighted the need for integrated surveys as there

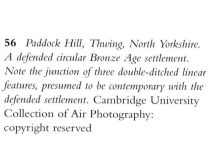

56 *Paddock Hill, Thwing, North Yorkshire. A defended circular Bronze Age settlement. Note the junction of three double-ditched linear features, presumed to be contemporary with the defended settlement.* Cambridge University Collection of Air Photography: copyright reserved

Later features

Bank

Ditch

N

0   30m

57 *The excavation plan of Paddock Hill, Thwing, a Bronze Age settlement. The outlying ditches are not Bronze Age and there is evidence of Anglo-Saxon occupation.* Copyright Yorkshire Archaeology Society and English Heritage

58 *Lea Green, Grassington, North Yorkshire. A Late Iron Age and Romano-British enclosure with associated field systems enhanced by a light covering of snow. Other features date from later industrial activities.* Cambridge University Collection of Air Photographs: copyright reserved

are a number of well-preserved sites and landscapes which are not yet fully understood. Fortunately, Andrew Fleming's work in Swaledale has been published (see further reading) which provides a better understanding of the prehistoric (and later) exploitations of the Dales. For the Bronze Age the initial stone clearance cairns are still visible, as are coaxial field systems; his interpretation of how people used this landscape is that they were predominantly concerned with livestock, with only garden-sized plots for crops. The soils were thin to start with, but after clearance and wetter conditions towards the end of the Bronze Age, peat growth takes over. This sequence makes fieldwork anywhere in the Pennines very difficult and thus the discovery of settlements particularly challenging.

Further north in Northumberland and southern Scotland there have been surveys and excavations by RCHME and Newcastle University. Standrop Rigg was excavated by George Jobey and proved to be a Bronze Age settlement. The dominant settlement type is the unenclosed settlement – houses, palisades but no encircling ditches, with fields beyond. Environmental evidence shows little indication of Bronze Age clearance, hence the small and unenclosed settlement pattern in this part of the north-east. The unenclosed settlement was a common form of site, often attributed to the Bronze Age, and excavations at Black Law and Standrop Rigg have confirmed this (59).

A new type of agriculture has been found, a narrow system of ploughing called cord rig (60). This type of cultivation has been dated mainly to the Iron Age but there is much more work which needs to be done on these palisaded sites and their fields in the Borders region. Recent work by Peter Topping at Linhope Burn has helped place cord rig and associated settlement in a first-millennium context.

Further north in Perthshire there have been recent surveys which have recorded the densest concentrations of prehistoric settlement in Scotland in the form of hut circles (61, 62). A total of 845 hut circles has been recorded in heather moorland often at altitudes higher than one would expect, at 300m to 400m (1,000-1,300ft). There has been little excavation of these features but the limited work that has been done shows that they date from the second millennium and early part of the first millennium.

59 *Standrop Rigg, Linhope, Northumberland. A late Bronze Age settlement with field systems.* After Jobey

60 *Woden Law, Roxburghshire. palisaded settlement and cord rigg, (narrow ridges formed as a result of ploughing).* Photo Tim Gates: Copyright Reserved RCHME, NT 7612/2

61 *Alyth Burn, Perthshire. Aerial photograph of circular houses forming prehistoric open settlements.* Crown Copyright: Royal Commission on the Ancient and Historical Monuments of Scotland

62 *Plan of the prehistoric houses at Alyth Burn, Perthshire.* Crown Copyright: Royal Commission on the Ancient and Historical Monuments of Scotland

Stonehenge and other sites

It had been my intention not to mention Stonehenge to any great degree in this book; but for a number of reasons it is worth mentioning. Stonehenge is not just interesting in terms of the stones and the henge, it is also important for the landscape in which it is set. On figure **64** there are many black lines and these refer to archaeological sites of one form or another; if this particular part of what is now Salisbury Plain was so heavily used in the Neolithic and Bronze Age for a variety of purposes, where were the people living? There are indications of settlements within a 3km (1.9 miles) radius of Stonehenge – on Rox Hill to the south and nearer, at the Winterbourne Crossroads. Both areas have field systems which may date from the Bronze Age; they are linked by a series of linear earthworks (in parts levelled), perhaps a boundary defining a territory for controlling livestock. These linear earthworks appear to meet on the top of spur on Wilsford Down; reminiscent of many other similar linear features throughout Wessex and as far north as the Wolds in east Yorkshire (**63**, **64**).

A Bronze Age occupation site has been found in Winterbourne Stoke at the Longbarrow Cross Roads (when the roundabout was being constructed). This site was probably an enclosed settlement, associated with the field system; the site as excavated contained four circular huts, three of which are illustrated here in plan (**64**). Julian Richards warns of the difficulty of finding Bronze Age settlements in Wessex; the increased use of bronze meant that the flint tools, which are so useful in finding Neolithic sites, are not only fewer in number but also not as diagnostic as the specialised flint-knapping of the Neolithic. Therefore when poor-quality flint tools are found they are harder to date and assign the flint scatters a Bronze Age settlement interpretation. There are a number of possible occupation sites in the Stonehenge area according to the RCHME's Stonehenge 1979 survey. The one mentioned in Winterbourne Stoke is 2.3km (1.4 miles) from Stonehenge itself. There is another, south of the ritual enclosure, Woodhenge, 3km (1.8 miles) north-east of Stonehenge. This site was discovered through excavation by Mrs Cunnington in the 1920s but the whole extent of the site was not revealed until the drought years of 1976; it is an egg-shaped enclosure with a trackway leading from it; the excavations indicate domestic activity from a number of pits which contained pottery and animal bones.

In the chalk landscape of Stonehenge there will have been a large amount of soil movement off the tops and slopes of the downs. Within the small dry valleys, sites may have been hidden and will remain preserved until research or a pipeline is required to disturb them. When you visit Stonehenge, now or in ten years, do not concentrate solely on the Stones and the Henge; imagine yourself in a landscape which has grown up over many centuries (even by the Bronze Age the landscape had been used for thousands of years); make the time to walk around the perimeter of the landscape, as it will help your understanding of the *scale* of 'prehistoric landscapes'. The landscape may seem very localised through modern eyes, but it is still broad enough to allow for a variety of activities to take place. In the Stonehenge landscape there is a 3km (1.9 mile) long *cursus* – was it a horse racing track? There is the henge itself with an avenue leading into it which undulates with the contours of the down; and many barrows which are visible from a number of places (**63**).

The whole landscape at Stonehenge is undergoing enormous change, not just the removal of the roads but also the reversion of many areas to pasture. The area has been surveyed and re-surveyed over the past 30 years and new information is revealed each time, not least by NMP projects. The most recent development has been a survey using a laser beam, using Lidar (Light Detection and Ranging) equipment; the laser beam records the surface of the ground, or vegetation (trees) or buildings. The results of this survey will be published soon (by the author and other colleagues) but they show new information on sites and field systems, as the Lidar is not dependent upon any lighting conditions or particular ground conditions. These discoveries are significant; if Lidar produces results in the Stonehenge landscape, one of the most surveyed areas of Britain if not Europe, the potential for discovering many new sites using this technique is high (**65**).

63 *Stonehenge area. Detail area around Wilsford Down showing junction of linear features settlements and barrows.* Crown Copyright NMR

Round barrows ● ●
Disc barrow ◎
Long barrow ●
levelled ○
Bank ----
Ditch ----
N
0   1km

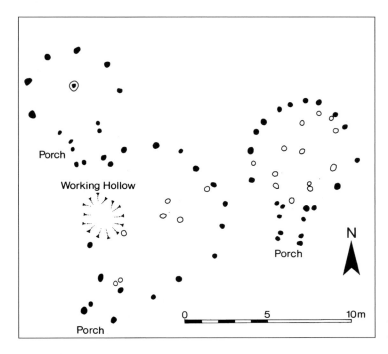

Porch

Working Hollow

Porch

Porch

N
0   5   10m

64 *Winterbourne Stoke, near Stonehenge, plans of houses from a prehistoric settlement*

65 *The Stonehenge landscape from the air, taken by USAF on Christmas Eve 1943.*
Crown copyright, NMR

Stonehenge may be the most well-known of prehistoric sites but Flag Fen is rapidly becoming one of the best Bronze Age visitor attractions. This is a waterlogged-wood, wet site with good preservation of wood and artefacts. There are reconstructed round houses, species of sheep similar to those in the Bronze Age and a brand new visitor centre. The site is currently under excavation as well as having good presentation to the public. The aerial photograph (**colour plate 10**) does remind us of the three-dimensional nature of archaeology; the yellow linear feature which runs away from the reconstructed lake is a Roman road, which sits above the waterlogged wood at Flag Fen. There are few better examples of the intensity of land-use over the past 5,000 years than around the fen-edge at Flag Fen.

6

IRON AGE SETTLEMENT

One of the main distorting factors and debates in Iron Age studies concerns the Celts. We cannot be divorced from the times we live in; there is today a huge political movement towards a closer, unified Europe. Recently the Celts have been promoted as a pan-European people, who, while enjoying a good fight, were talented, artistic and a thoroughly 'good thing'. The *I Celti* exhibition in Venice, television programmes, large edited volumes (see Miranda Green's *The Celtic World*) and colour supplement articles keep the momentum going so that we can understand the last 2,000 years of history in the context of its foundations in prehistory. The Celts have been used as a legitimating force for a unified Europe. A peaceful, unified Europe is clearly beneficial for its future but it is difficult to use the Celts as a model. If peace is the goal, using a warrior-based society such as the Celts is not necessarily the best example.

For the first time in the prehistoric period we have a closer insight into the nature of the people, their names, their beliefs and way of life; it is a form of proto-history rather than just prehistory. We have coinage and written sources, especially from those making contact with these barbarian tribes, who give their comments on the Celts.

> Celtic . . . is a magic bag, into which anything may be put, and out of which almost anything may come . . . . Anything is possible in the fabulous Celtic twilight, which is not so much a twilight of the gods as of the reason.
>
> J.R.R. Tolkien, 1963, 'English and Welsh'.
> in *Angles and Britons*, Cardiff, University of
> Wales Press. O'Donnell Lectures.

In contrast to the preceding periods it is settlements, not burials, which characterise Iron Age Britain; this is not exclusively so, but in comparison to the previous periods the number of hillforts and the sheer number of enclosures (some of which have been excavated) have given us a clear picture of population growth in the first millennium BC. This final millennium of prehistory saw the transition from the ranching farmers of the Bronze Age and the beginning of what we loosely term the Iron Age. These 800 years are famous for hillforts, farmsteads, earthworks and cropmarks of enclosures with round houses, field systems, brochs, crannogs and so much data that few people have ventured to attempt synthesis. One who has, Professor Barry Cunliffe of Oxford University, has written the standard text and any reader who wishes to pursue this subject should read his *Iron Age Communities in Britain*. This is not to say that his interpretations are accepted uncritically, and Iron Age studies, perhaps more than any part of prehistoric archaeology, are characterised by deep divisions between academics. This is in fact good for the subject, and need not concern us here. The point of mentioning it is to reinforce the point that there is no 'right' or 'wrong' interpretation in archaeology; only the latest fashion and the standard orthodoxy. The fashions of the current decade will become the standard orthodoxy of the next.

As in all archaeology, Iron Age studies are moving away from the 'famous site' (Danebury, Maiden Castle and Glastonbury) and beginning to examine the 'landscape'. Another interesting approach is that of looking at what Iron Age people did not leave behind as well as trying to understand settlements from what was left behind. As we have seen in the Mesolithic, the information in middens provides us with detailed information of human behaviour. If we imagine that we suddenly deserted, or even deliberately cleared out, our current houses and settlements, what would we leave for the archaeologists of the future? There would be an abundance of information about the house and its construction but little about the people who lived there, what they ate and how they behaved. As we will see later, it is the lack of 'rubbish' on many sites which has been overlooked. While we often say how much information we have for the Iron Age, this is only true in comparison with the Neolithic and Bronze Ages.

A recent article begins with the phrase 'the Iron Age is boring'; it is posed as a question rather than a statement and in reality the Iron Age is perhaps one of the most interesting times to study. There is such a wealth of information relating to the sites in the Iron Age which reveal their way of life in some detail. By the time of the Romans' arrival, coinage and writing have been introduced and some organisation can be seen amongst the tribes, which we can name, thanks to Caesar (**66**).

Iron Age settlement is a huge subject which cannot be easily condensed, so only a flavour can be presented here, taking a few examples from a variety of locations. Iron Age studies reflect the history of archaeology in general; initially high-status sites were subject to campaigns of excavation by high-status archaeologists (Sir Mortimer Wheeler excavating at Maiden Castle and

66 *The location and names of Iron Age tribes, according to Julius Caesar*

Professor Barry Cunliffe at Danebury for example). This attitude reflects the single-site approach which has traditionally been the start of many archaeological studies, but understanding how sites functioned in a landscape context is becoming much more common. The most visible sites (large earthworks on hilltops), like the round barrows of the Bronze Age, were the focus of attention until the study of landscapes became possible with aerial photography and more extensive fieldwork programmes.

It is instructive to look at the excavations of farmsteads; the first one was in 1938 under very unusual circumstances at Little Woodbury (**67**, **68**) by Gerhard Bersu (a German 'refugee', who was eventually 'interned' on the Isle of Man for the duration of the Second World War); the next excavation was not until 1960 with the excavation at Pimperne, Dorset (and Longridge Deverill Cow Down). Woodbury was published in *Proceedings of the Prehistoric Society* for 1940 and Pimperne (same internal area as Danebury hillfort) was not published until 1993 (**69**). Both excavations had a profound effect on the

67 *Plan of the Iron Age enclosures at Woodbury and Little Woodbury in relation to the cultivation system on estate maps of c.1600 and 1703 (broken black)*

way in which the Iron Age was understood for two generations. Woodbury became the name of a 'type of culture' and the Pimperne house was the basis for a reconstructed round house at Butser Hill. The Butser experiment has been one of the most sustained archaeological scientific studies undertaken this century in this country and has maintained a high public profile throughout. A visit to Butser is essential for understanding prehistoric settlement (**colour plate 14**). Other places where there are reconstructed round houses and prehistoric activities are Castel Henlyss and Flag Fen (see places to visit).

Hillforts

A few hilltops were defended in the Neolithic – Carn Brea and Crickley Hill, Windmill Hill, Hambledon Hill, Maiden Castle and possibly Carrock Fell. For 2,000 years there was little sign of fortification, until the end of the second millennium BC and a number of hilltops were defended or protected by ramparts and ditches – sometimes palisades e.g. Norton Fitzwarren (Somerset), Rams Hill (Berkshire) and later at the Briedden (Powys). In eastern England from Yorkshire to Kent a number of ring forts have been excavated, for example Paddock Hill (Thwing) (**56**). Springfield Lyons (Essex), and Mucking (Essex), show they contained a few circular houses and judging from the high-status objects, were perhaps fortified homesteads.

The construction of Iron Age hillforts indicates a change in the organisation of society. Early interpretations favoured an invasion of new people who brought iron with them. But was this what happened? Trade and contacts were growing and these early explanations of how society changed seemed too simplistic.

Excavators at Maiden Castle (**8, 70**) reflect the changes in twentieth-century theories. Sir Mortimer Wheeler, who excavated there in the 1930s, was of the invasion theory school. In the 1980s English Heritage arranged a large scale re-evaluation at Maiden Castle and the excavator, Niall Sharples, espouses an altogether less simplistic view. He argues that the invasion hypothesis assumes a relatively static model for all societies, and this has been shown to not be the case. Work over the last 30 years, by anthropologists and sociologists, has shown that all societies are dynamic and are always changing. Often this change is imperceptible in the archaeological record, but the major changes are recoverable.

68 *Little Woodbury as photographed by O.G.S. Crawford, with the excavation trench outlined in white.* Crown Copyright NMR, SU 1427/13/IA

69 *The excavation of the round house at Pimperne, Dorset.* Copyright I.M. Blake and D.W. Harding

70 *Maiden Castle, Dorset. One of the most impressive Iron Age hillforts in England.* Crown Copyright NMR SY 6688/113

Sharples' theory is that the desire for change amongst the Bronze Age people, in which trade networks were established, and in which bronze was fundamental, could also be achieved through the introduction of iron; especially if there was a growing population not all of whom could control the trade or production of bronze. New sources and new networks could be built up to the exclusion of the old 'bronze' system. Technological developments are often the catalyst for change and, although we might never fully understand the mechanics of the change from bronze to iron, the manifestation (new settlements in prominent places) is easy to record. It is also apparent that the population increased in certain areas; it is not just that we find it difficult to locate Bronze Age settlements in comparison to Iron Age ones. There are many more Iron Age settlements and therefore we must conclude there was a much larger population which had a well-organised structure.

The term 'hillfort' as a class of monument is like any grouping – an oversimplification and a handy label. The term hillfort refers to any ancient (presumed prehistoric, pre-Roman) enclosure on a hilltop or similar location. The ditches and ramparts can be large and numerous earthworks as at Maiden Castle (**70**), or slighter single stone works. By using the term hillfort we are assuming a defended place, probably to protect a settlement. A common theme of early twentieth-century interpretations saw hillforts as refuges in times of crisis; a clarion call would be sounded and all the farmers and families would down tools and rush up to the hilltop in advance of an attack. This was the image I had instilled into me from an early age (or I dreamt it up myself!). This was a favourite interpretation for Carrock Fell (**colour plate 8**) as the Romans built at least three military camps within 7km (4.4 miles) of the hillfort. No doubt some of the hillforts in the country did fulfil this role but there are many other possible interpretations.

Hillforts as a class of site did develop through time; not just as a proliferation of sites but also a development in size, shape, number of ramparts and ditches, entrance design and function. In this way they are a reflection of the society of the time.

There are over 1,350 hillforts in England excluding those in Cumbria, Northumberland, Durham, Cleveland, and the Isle of Man. These latter areas have superb hillforts, even if they are few in number (**71**). The main syntheses of hillforts have concentrated on those in England and Wales. They have been classified into two main categories of forts – 'promontory' and 'contour', with two sub-divisions for each category of 'hill-slope fort' and 'plateau fort'. These

71 *The distribution of Iron Age hillforts in England (produced from information provided by the NMR).* English Heritage

72 *Segsbury hillfort, Berkshire. Geophysical plot and interpretation.* English Heritage

are self-explanatory terms but they do beg the question of the overall label 'hillfort'. Clearly there is a difference between a defended enclosure on a 'hill slope' and a 'hilltop'; although there may better terms than 'hillfort' it is so commonly accepted that to attempt to change it would be difficult. The problem here is with the overall label and for convenience the term hillfort has to be used, as long as it is understood that some sites in this category are not forts and are not on hills!

Another method of dividing up these sites is by size and location and in James Dyer's Shire Archaeology book on hillforts this is what he has done. There are hillforts which date from the eighth to sixth century BC which he describes as hilltop enclosures, 6-20ha (15-50 acres) in extent, with four-post buildings and circular huts inside (**72**); they often have weak defences, a good example is Norbury camp in Gloucestershire. Another category is the fortified enclosures: strongly defended with timber and stone, sometimes with two ditches (bivallate) and sited on the end of prominent spurs and ridges, and 2-4ha (5-10 acres) in size. Their strategic location is important and they are usually later than the hilltop enclosures. Good examples would be Lidbury camp in Wiltshire, or Caer Caradoc, near Chapel Lawn in Shropshire.

The main period of hillfort construction was in the sixth to fourth centuries BC with contour and plateau forts, approximately 5ha (12 acres) in extent, with timber or stone-faced ramparts and a 'V'-shaped ditch. The general interpretation is that local chieftains were in conflict with each other and defended centres were necessary. They were also a symbol of power and some of these hillforts became developed hillforts; well defended, with multiple ramparts – Maiden Castle, Hod Hill (**79**) and Danebury. Maiden Castle and Hod Hill were attacked by Vespasian in AD 43. Suetonius chronicled Vespasian's life (he became Emperor in AD 69) and describes how in thirty battles he subdued two powerful tribes and twenty hillforts in southern England.

The extent to which hillforts were built in response to the Roman invasion is a matter for debate but it is interesting to note that at Hod Hill, one corner of the hillfort has been converted into a Roman fort. **Colour plate 11** shows a reconstruction of the more developed type of hillfort.

It has been suggested that certain hillforts cannot have been defended (Scratchbury in Wiltshire) because the whole of the interior is visible from below. (This gives any would-be attacker the distinct advantage of being able to see any defensive deployments.) So if defence was not the primary purpose what was the function of the site? One theory is that from a highly visible monument, certain activities would take place which spectators (outside) could see, but not intrude upon or intervene. The exact location of Scratchbury, for example, suggests a procession of some sort (not an uncommon practice earlier in prehistory given the 'avenues' at Avebury, Stonehenge and in the Millfield basin). Scratchbury has a number of barrows adjacent to it with a circular enclosure beyond the barrows along the ridge top. Perhaps these enclosures were ceremonial centres, at least for part of their existence.

Hillforts have usually been assumed to represent a society based on tribal chiefs (**73**). This has been questioned recently and the excavations in the Fens

73 *Hillforts in Wessex with theoretical territories based on Thiessen polygons.* After Cunliffe

at Wardy Hill, Coveney (**colour plate 12**) have been used to add to the debate. The paucity of Iron Age occupation in the Fens has been commented on since the 1920s; the lack of an Iron Age population was thought to be either risk of infection from malaria (given the wet conditions) or the accelerated population growth in the neighbouring fertile uplands. The environment (topography) has to be understood at a local scale especially in the fens; every minor hillock and ancient water course (**74**) would have its significance. The known Iron Age sites south of the Fens are all univallate and circular (**75**), whilst those in the fen are much more complex. Wardy Hill ringwork (**colour plate 12**) on a spur of Ampthill clay on the north side of

74 *The Landscape of the Fens from the air. The ancient river system and creeks (called roddons) can be seen as lighter marks with the recent drainage pattern and rectilinear modern fields superimposed on this landscape between Peterborough and Chatteris.* Cambridge University Collection of Air Photographs: copyright reserved

114

75 *Belsar's Hill, ringwork in the lowlands of Cambridgeshire. Note the way in which the medieval field system has used the ramparts of the hillfort.* Photograph by Chris Cox

the Isle of Ely, seems to be of the developed kind of hillfort and is situated 6m (20ft) above OD. This siting has been described as 'strategic', as 6m (20ft) represented the difference between dry land and being submerged! Our understanding of the Iron Age population in the Fens has improved as a result of intensive surveys (using aerial photographs and fieldwork), and although a difficult environment to control, it is clear it was an important area for settlement of Iron Age communities.

The form of the site is such that had it been an earthwork on a similarly strategic hill elsewhere it would have been an important hillfort. The results of the excavations at Wardy Hill have shown that it is probably a high–status site but the cause of its abandonment probably led to the occupants taking their wealth with them. As the excavator Chris Evans states in an interim report,

> It is essential we consider what would have been in involved in the abandonment of a site when faced with rising water levels. This is not a matter of Atlantis like incidence; it would entail a period of cognitive assessment leading to a decision to pack-up one's worldly goods and move. At Wardy Hill we did not recover swords, shield, cart fittings, nor other readily accepted markers of Iron Age social hierarchy. Yet, given the abandonment scenario as outlined above, one would not expect to.

This theme of what was left behind and site-formation processes will be picked up later.

As the hillfort developed it is easier to see its function as a defended place, like a walled town (foreshadowing the later *oppida*, see below), operating as a centralised distribution centre, military barracks or protected farmstead. It played an important part in Iron Age society and continues to do so today as a refuge for people to escape their twentieth-century settlements.

Questions on how long it took to build a hillfort are difficult to answer as the local conditions would affect this greatly. An average guess is 200 men would take four months, at a time of stress, but what caused this stress? Was it as a result of immigration or population expansion? Archaeologists cannot agree on this but there is a huge amount of evidence for the expansion of farming which does indicate an increase in population, especially in the last centuries before the Roman invasion.

Hillforts about 6ha (15 acres) in size were constructed in Dorset during the early Iron Age. They had self-sufficient communities with sizeable grain storage facilities; control of land rather than status (status was defined by trade for bronze shields and swords in the Bronze Age) was the way forward in the Iron Age's new economy. Defended sites with rich agricultural land were the power base for local chiefs. Maiden Castle developed more than others because it was well placed to exploit these local resources. Control of people in the Iron Age was through land, produce and storage. This is perhaps too appropriate as a model for the capitalist world in which we live, and it therefore has to be questioned, but the evidence does point to a strong ruling class.

Maiden Castle developed from 450 BC; the area enclosed by the hillfort increased from 6.5ha (16 acres) to 19ha (47 acres) taking in the area on the hilltop to the west of the existing hillfort. The only comparable site is Hambledon (**30**) which began in the Neolithic (see causewayed camps above) but in the Iron Age increased to 8.1ha (20 acres) and then again to 12.5ha (30 acres). Other hillforts expanded in size in Dorset but they were further apart than the smaller ones; surely a clear suggestion of territorial and tribal control. The smaller hillforts may have been abandoned at this time and their communities incorporated into the lowland external settlements. Sharples suggests that the occupants of the Early Iron Age site at Poundbury moved to Maiden Castle and forced the occupants of Chalbury hillfort to abandon their defence in favour of undefended lowland settlements. If this was a result of warfare, there is little evidence for an armed conflict.

Hambledon Hill (**30**) is the only other hillfort to achieve anything like the status which Maiden Castle achieved. It appears that Hambledon Hill was abandoned during the middle Iron Age and the occupants moved to Hod Hill (**79, 80**). Hod Hill had originally been occupied in the Bronze Age but was abandoned when Hambledon Hill was occupied. Only when expansion was necessary at Hambledon Hill and more space required, was Hod Hill re-occupied. It was in use in 43 AD, when many of the Durotrigian forts (the *Durotriges* were the local tribe) were attacked by Vespasian.

Apart from the impressive earthwork defences of banks and ditches those hillforts which have had been partially excavated reveal some interesting internal details. A very common feature is the 'four poster', a square or rectangular arrangement of four post-holes. These are regular features inside hillforts in England and Wales, but are they houses, are they storage, or exposure platforms for the dead? Are they watch towers or granaries? The latter interpretation is the most likely if the point about control of land and food is correct.

One of the most striking landmarks in central southern England is the Uffington White Horse, situated on a north-facing chalk slope of the Lambourn Downs. It is surrounded by archaeological sites which have been investigated recently, not least the hillfort, Uffington Castle (**colour plate 25**), the horse itself and a site in the valley below. This low-lying site was recorded from the air, subject to a geophysical survey and small-scale excavation. Using optical stimulated luminescence dating (OSL) sediments associated with the earliest horse (as there have been many re-cuts of the horse itself) indicate that the horse is at least 2,500 years old, and thus may be Early Iron Age or even Late Bronze Age. This could be contemporaneous with the first phase of the hillfort and the first phase of the low-lying settlement (**76, 77**). It is worth speculating that the inhabitants of the settlement may have been the builders of the Horse and the hillfort; from the location of the settlement there is one of the best views of the horse, apart from being in the air (**76, 77**). (I am grateful to Alan Hardy of Oxford Archaeology for supplying this information prior to publication).

The distribution of hillforts in Wales has been published by Chris Musson (**78**) in his report of his excavations at the Breiddin hillfort. Apart from the density of hillforts it is interesting to see the size distinctions, with smaller forts

76 *Uffington Museum site, near White Horse Hill. Transcription from aerial photographs.* English Heritage

0 —————— 45m

-1.45 -0.28 nT 0.88 2.05

N

0 ▬▬▬▬▬▬▬ 90m

77 *Uffington Museum site, near White Horse Hill. Geophysical plot.* English Heritage

in the south and west and a series of large and larger forts in the Marches, between Wales and England. One particularly impressive site is Tre'r Ceiri, on the Lleyn peninsula (**81**). This is a large defensive village within double stone ramparts with numerous stone-built hut circles inside, and is reckoned to date from the last few centuries before the Roman conquest and continuing into the first millennium AD.

Before leaving hillforts, there are the stone-built hillforts of northern England and Scotland. Yeavering, on the summit of Yeavering Bell in Northumberland (**82**), surrounds the top of a steep hill and encloses an earlier Bronze Age cairn, clearly visible on the aerial photograph. On the slopes of the hill there are a number of other features, enclosures and fields which are presumed to be contemporary with the hillfort. The date of the hillfort is uncertain but it is presumed to be Iron Age.

Another striking example of a northern hillfort is on the summit of Ingleborough in the Yorkshire Dales near Ingleton (**83** and **colour plate 26**). This magnificent setting for a hillfort incorporates a stone rampart which

78 *The distribution of Iron Age hillforts in Wales. Produced from information provided by C. Musson*

Hillforts under 1·2 ha
Hillforts 1·2–6 ha
Hillforts over 6 ha

HOD HILL, STOURPAINE

ONE ACRE

C BANK OR SCARF
C DITCH
▪ MOUND
• PIT

SCALE

79 *Hod Hill, Dorset. An Iron Age hillfort and Roman fort; note the hut circles in the south-east quadrant which have not been ploughed; see also the aerial photograph.* Crown Copyright, NMR

80 *Hod Hill, Dorset. Iron Age hillfort and Roman fort from the air.* Crown Copyright, NMR ST 2510/45/205

81 *Tre'r Ceiri hillfort on Lleyn peninsula, Wales. Its commanding position overlooking fertile land and the coast led to a long occupation of the hilltop from the prehistoric through to the late Roman period.* Cambridge University Collection of Air Photographs: copyright reserved

82 *Yeavering Bell, Northumberland, topped by a Bronze Age cairn and stone-built hillfort.* Crown Copyright NMR NT 9229/10/53

encircles most of the summit and a number of stone rings which are presumed to be the stone foundations for houses. This site is worth visiting but the only threat to it is from those who visit and add stones to the large (modern) cairn; the stones are often from sensitive archaeological structures – so if you do visit 'take only photographs, leave only footprints and kill only time' to quote from the sign at another hillfort, Crickley Hill in Gloucestershire.

The Iron Age round house

Perhaps the most common feature of the Iron Age is the round house (**85 & colour plate 21**). Examples of these are found on virtually every Iron Age site be it a hillfort or a small farmstead. The round house was the everyday living quarter of the family in the Iron Age; its size was dependent on the status of the occupant but it was where the cooking, eating, socialising and sleeping took place on Iron Age sites. If you visit Butser Ancient Farm in Hampshire (**colour plate 14**) you will see a reconstruction of a large Iron Age house (from Longridge Deverill Cow Down). The floor area of this house is over 205m^2 (2,000ft^2) and it is immediately apparent that this size of house would have been an important focus on any site. There are also two smaller houses reconstructed (based on evidence from Glastonbury) and these were probably for keeping stock in (if the high phosphate levels from another round house, at Moel-y-Gaer, really does represent the remains of manure). The contrast in size between these types of round house (with apparently no intermediate size) is not only noticeable but also not fully understood.

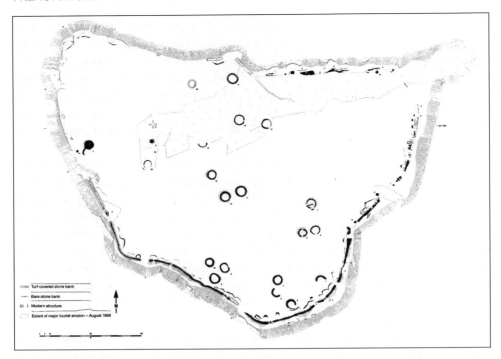

83 *Plan of the hillfort at Ingleborough, North Yorkshire. The stone ramparts and over 20 hut circles are very fragile; note the area of erosion (dashed line) caused by visitors removing stones from the hut circles and adding them to the 'walkers' cairn'.* Crown Copyright, NMR

The round house structure is a cone supported by a cylinder, with the outer wall a ring of posts with wattle and daub (clay) between the posts. Often there was an inner ring of posts for supporting the roof. It has been noted that the doorway of the large round houses is unusually large, more like a barn door than a house door; it is possible that wagons were used to bring in material which could have been stored in the area in the 'cone' of the roof. The roof would have been at a 45° angle making the apex of the roof 8m (25ft) above the ground. The roof would have been made from rafters which would have been thatched. The structural techniques and details of roofing and thatching are well presented at both the Buster Ancient Farm, Chalton, Hampshire for the Iron Age and at Flag Fen, near Peterborough for the Bronze Age.

In social terms we know very little about the round house. One theory is that the space within the house could have been divided into two; the middle (central) area which was the 'public' space and the outer ring (between the inner ring and the outer wall) being the 'private' space. This theory is influenced by the structuralist philosophies of Lévi-Strauss in which binary oppositions of public and private, or male and female, cooked and raw, are used as explanatory tools, but they may not have operated in the Iron Age (or any 'Age' for that matter). It is unfortunate that with so many anthropological studies about houses and communities we do not have better developed theories about the Iron Age round houses. The public and private dichotomy is a starting point but with properly oriented research excavations it may be possible to learn more about the way in which all the aspects of Iron Age societies functioned. We are not really clear about the organisation on a daily or annual basis. Reference has been made to the *sunwise model* in the Bronze Age section but it was devised from evidence in the larger Iron Age houses of Wessex.

Recent research has shown that the entrances of Iron Age round houses have a tendency (**84**) to be oriented towards midsummer sunrise and the autumn equinox (north-east through east to south-east). This has led to the suggestion of splitting the use of space within the house along an east-west axis. The evidence from Longridge Deverill Cow Down round house (which was burnt down) shows that the left (south side) of the house contained large quantities of occupational debris whereas the right (north side) of the house was devoid of any occupational debris. Mike Parker Pearson and Colin Richards also argue that this east-west dichotomy is evident in most settlement enclosures and if the enclosures have a north-south divide they are not settlements.

This suggestion needs further investigation and detailed analysis but it provides a hypothesis which can be tested by a number of projects which are currently taking place in England, which involve mapping all archaeological sites from the air, part of English Heritage's National Mapping Programme (NMP). The orientation of the entrance of each enclosure is being recorded. Another

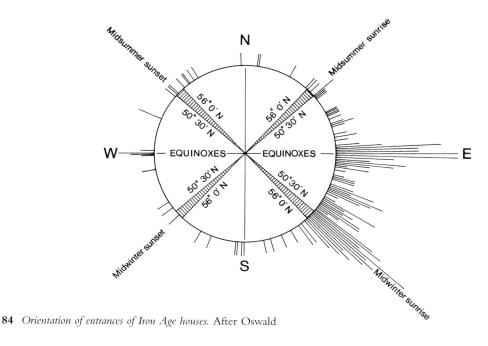

84 *Orientation of entrances of Iron Age houses. After Oswald*

Iron-Age House A1, Carn Euny, Cornwall.

85 *Reconstruction of life in a round house at Carn Euny, Cornwall.* English Heritage. Judith Dobie

contribution NMP is making to our understanding of Iron Age society is in the number of prehistoric enclosures being recorded. Often it is difficult to assess the date other than 'prehistoric' but many more have been found in Cornwall, where the predominant Iron Age settlement is a 'round' (usually a circular enclosure, but a few square enclosures, or square 'rounds' have been interpreted as Iron Age). This increase in number, almost by 30 per cent, making a total of nearly 1,500 sites, dramatically alters our perceptions of the levels of population in the Iron Age. In terms of distribution, if randomly spaced, this means there will be a settlement every five or six kilometres; in reality the distribution is not random and there are many clusters of sites, with open areas in between. Research into the distribution of these enclosures is just beginning, and in particular, into the relationship with soils types and the landscapes zones (as characterised by the Historic Landscape Characterisation projects funded by English Heritage).

The question of the roles of men, women and children in prehistoric society is often asked. Did they have particular roles as anthropological studies suggest they should do? Some would argue archaeological techniques are not capable of throwing more light on these questions. This may be so, but it should not deter us from attempting to find out. As mentioned above, recent work by J.D. Hill on site formation processes and the Iron Age highlights a significant weakness in the information we obtain from Iron Age sites; the lack of domestic rubbish is surprising but seems to be true.

For example in the early Iron Age phase at Winnal Down one pit was filled every 7-10 years (based on the excavated data); only one rim sherd would have been lost every 9-12 months, given a 200-year occupation! If an Iron Age pot weighed 1kg and only 25.8kg were found then this is not a representative sample of Iron Age pottery; where has it gone? At Danebury a loom weight or comb would have been lost every two years given the number recovered from the excavations; similarly there are only 100 identifiable bone fragments a year, from a population estimated to be between 250 and 500 people. So, although it might be stretching a point to say the sites are 'clean', the amount of rubbish which 200 people leave per year was obviously being removed from the site and our interpretations will have to reflect this bias.

Future studies will have to involve the density of settlement within the hillfort or farmstead. Suggestions have been made of 15 persons per acre inside a hillfort; others say this is too high and others too low. Another proposal is 25 persons per acre. If we take the lowest figure then for Maiden Castle at its height there would have been over 700 people living there. It is difficult to know how correct this is especially given the fact that a hillfort such as Maiden Castle was more than just a place to live.

So often in archaeology we present information about sites or landscapes which seem complete and whole; we forget that we are dealing with human behaviour and the results of success and failure. Ladle Hill in Hampshire is a good example of what has been described as an 'unfinished hillfort'; the banks (**86, 87**) appear to be no more than the dumped upcast from the ditches. The causes for such a circumstance can only be guessed at, but the site has other interesting features. The linear earthworks and rectangular enclosures which can be seen on the aerial photograph (**87**) are evidence of organising a landscape for pasture and cattle herding. The linear earthworks may be earlier than the hillfort.

Danebury (**88, 89**) is one the most famous of all Iron Age hillforts but it is its landscape on which I want to dwell. The hillfort was excavated over 20 seasons, finishing in 1988 with over half the defended area being excavated.

86 *An early aerial photograph of Ladle Hill, Hampshire, an Iron Age hillfort.* Crown Copyright, NMR SU 4756/11

87 *Ladle Hill showing the associated linear features (middle right especially) and Bronze Age barrows.*
Crown Copyright, NMR, SU4756/66

But what about the 'landscape context' in which it was set? The work of
Rog Palmer analysing and interpreting aerial photographs of the surrounding
landscape formed the basis for the Danebury Environs Project (under the
direction of Professor Cunliffe). The results of this seven-year project (1989–
95), which examined the evolution of the landscape in the first millennium BC
and first millennium AD have now been published (see Cunliffe, Cunliffe and
Poole in further reading). The project produced very good results, showing the
increased complexity of Iron Age sites, as well as using latest survey techniques,
especially geophysical investigations (**92**, **93** and **94**) to improve our
understanding of what went on inside these sites (I am grateful to Andy Payne
of English Heritage for providing the geophysical survey plans). Professor
Cunliffe has written, 'It has been a salutary warning to those of us who like to
make generalising statements about Iron Age society that each of the field
work programmes has demanded significant readjustments to comfortable
preconceptions – how disorienting new data can be!'

88 *Danebury, Hampshire, from the air during the excavations in 1975.* Crown Copyright, NMR SU 4576/66

89 *Danebury area: an extract from a survey of aerial photographs showing the hillforts, field systems and barrows.* Crown Copyright NMR

Danebury

⊙ • Round barrows   ○ • Ring ditches   ●○ Oval barrow   0 _____ 1km

N

The work is setting the hillforts of Danebury, Woolbury and Bury Hill (**90**) in their landscape contexts. The landscape around Danebury is a complex pattern of linear boundaries and field systems (**89**), which have been revealed by aerial photography and more recently geophysics (**92**, **93**, and **94**) presented clearly by Rog Palmer in an RCHME survey (see further reading).

Farmsteads

The Iron Age is also characterised by a huge number of 'farmsteads'; these manifest themselves in a number of ways but they are most often seen as curvilinear and rectilinear cropmark sites, as already shown for Woodbury (**67**, **68**). There is a number of excellently preserved stone-built sites, and Carn Euny (**85**) is a very good example and well worth visiting, not least to crawl down the fogou (a subterranean chamber). The stone houses which are visible today are the later replacements of earlier wooden ones.

90 *Bury Hill, Hampshire. Interpretation of the internal features based on a geophysical survey.* Copyright English Heritage

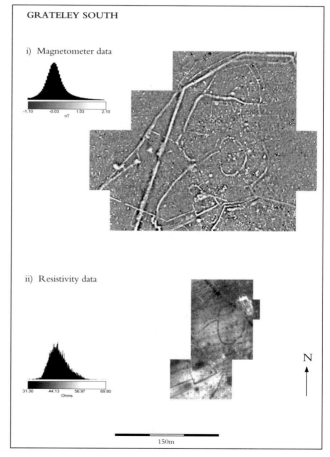

91 *Quarley Hill near Danebury, Hampshire. A hillfort with associated linear ditches which define an area without smaller fields but which may be contemporary with the small rectangular fields in the west.* Crown Copyright RCHME

92 *Geophysical surveys in the Danebury area. Grateley settlement which began in the Iron Age and developed as a farmstead (villa) in the Roman period.* English Heritage

GRATELEY SOUTH

i) Magnetometer data

ii) Resistivity data

150m

The distribution of Iron Age farmsteads has never been mapped but they are found throughout Britain in some form or other. A striking example of one which has been excavated is Thorpe Thewles in Cleveland. It was the largest open excavation of an Iron Age defended site in North England, which revealed two distinct occupation phases. The site started as a defended enclosure in 200 BC (**colour plate 15**) and then became an open settlement with internal partitions by AD 50. The economic base for the site was mixed farming with cattle being the predominant source of food. Sheep were also an important secondary resource for food and wool with pigs also being reared.

The reconstruction of Thorpe Thewles (**colour plate 15**) and another similar site, in Essex, known as the Airport Catering site, Stansted are perhaps the best medium for communicating what this type of Iron Age settlement looked like. Usually in excavation reports only the plan of the site (for example at Winnal Down in Hampshire) is used to show the layout of the sites, the ditches, round house and the distribution of selected artefacts.

93 *Geophysical surveys in Farm, Danebury area. Suddern farmstead, Early Iron Age farmstead, which continued in use in to the Roman period; notice the preponderance of pits.* English Heritage

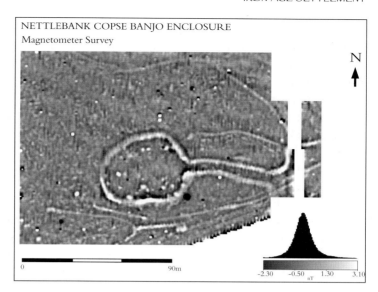

NETTLEBANK COPSE BANJO ENCLOSURE
Magnetometer Survey

N

0   90m

-2.30   -0.50   1.30   3.10
                  nT

94 *Geophysical surveys in Danebury area. Nettlebank Copse banjo enclosure; an Early Iron Age farmstead, probably for a single family unit*

The settlement history at Winnal Down goes back to the Neolithic, with an open settlement in the Bronze Age, which is replaced in the Early Iron Age by a D-shaped enclosure; the ditch of the enclosure was partially filled in the middle Iron Age and an open settlement established. Winnal Down was unlikely to have been a high-status site and could be described, like Thorpe Thewles, as the average Iron Age settlement. There is evidence for metalworking in the late phases, there are a few items of ornament and wealth but nothing exceptional. The wealth of its occupants will have been derived from woollen goods and livestock in the early Iron Age (as there seems to be some evidence for textiles), and from cereal production in the middle Iron Age.

Mention of Pimperne has already been made (**69**, **95**) and it is worth returning to the site and landscape around Pimperne. Survey work had revealed a landscape on the chalk which includes sites with which we are familiar (**95**) and also the more unusual (**96**). This site seems to be a developed form of the double-ditched enclosure with divisions in the outer enclosure; this may be to meet a particular need or function and seems to be related to cattle or stock control.

Through aerial photography archaeologists have been discovering not only new sites which are inevitably threatened when so near gravel pits as this one near Ashton Keynes, Wiltshire appears to be (**colour plate 13**), but also new classes of site; fortunately it is 'scheduled' which means it is protected from total destruction, by law. In Wales, Terry James has discovered a whole new class of site, which he has called 'concentric antenna enclosures' which are presumed to be Iron Age in date (**97**). The discovery of banjo enclosures during the 1990s, through aerial survey, has considerably expanded their distribution in southern

95 *Pimperne, Dorset. The excavated site is the one labelled T.H. (18) – see aerial photograph below. Note the juxtaposition of other sites and field systems.* Crown Copyright NMR

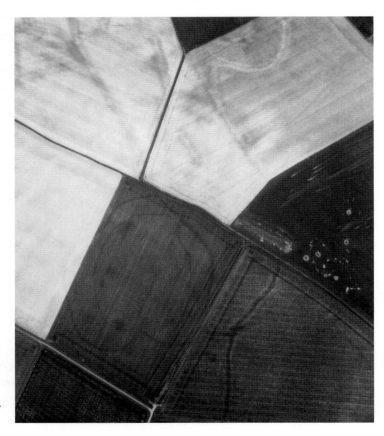

96 *Aerial photograph of Pimperne 18, Dorset.* Crown Copyright RCHME, ST 9110/41

England. The dry summers of 1995 and 1996, coupled with the opening up of airspace when the Upper Heyford airbase closed (one positive peace dividend at the end of the Cold War), produced an enormous increase in banjo and similar sites being recorded from the air in the Cherwell valley and environs by the former RCHME (now English Heritage) aerial reconnaissance team. In one year alone over 100 new sites were recorded (**colour plate 17**); further work is required to analyse these discoveries but their distribution, when mapped against soils is very revealing and begs the question of what the distribution means (**colour plate 17**). Were the sites located on the fertile, freer draining soils in the Iron Age or does the distribution reflect the ground conditions which produce these cropmark features?

Results of NMP have expanded our knowledge of banjo enclosures, this time on the chalk landscapes of the Lambourn Downs in Berkshire; here the fragmentary remains of field systems were shown to be masking earlier banjo enclosures. Analysis by Helen Winton (of English Heritage) has shown that there are some 12 banjo sites situated at the head of (now) dry valleys, with the funnel entrances pointing towards the valley bottoms (**colour plate 18**). This is perhaps indicative of cattle and sheep movements using the lower pastures for grazing and watering. Further work is required to understand the nature of the sites and the changes in the environment since the Iron Age, but these two examples show that we can never rely on distribution maps, as we have expanded the distribution of banjos in southern England.

Excavations at a more familiar type of site, in Wales, of a quadruple-ditched enclosure, at Collfryn (**98**, **99**), produced a series of Iron Age (and later) hut circles (**99**) and is good example of the way a site was used, abandoned and re-

97 *'Antenna enclosure' at Brechfa, Llandissilio, Wales, a new class of site; the 'antenna' is the outer ring.* After Terry James

0   100m

133

occupied; this site is one of many semi-defensive enclosures in the upper Severn valley in mid-Wales. The first enclosure was built in the third century BC and may have consisted of three encircling ditches, with a single entrance. From the finds it is likely to have been a reasonably high-status site with an extended-family group. At this time there were probably 3-4 roundhouses and 4-5 four-posters at any one time. The site was reduced in the first century BC to a double-ditched enclosure by re-cutting the original inner ditch and digging a new one immediately outside it. There was a mixed farming economy of cattle, sheep (or goat) and pig remains with those of glume wheats, barley and oats. Self-sufficiency was required in most daily needs including the making of bronze and iron tools. Pottery was rare in this area (as it was in the north of England in the Iron Age). Small-scale occupation at the site continued until the fourth century AD. This type of site is obviously a 'defended' farmstead, though what the defences were is a matter for debate.

98 *Collfryn, Wales: defended enclosure from the air.* Copyright: Clywd-Powys Archaeological Trust

99 *Collfryn, Wales, excavation plan.* Copyright: Clywd-Powys Archaeological Trust

The concept of families defending and enclosing their homes begins in the late second millennium and has continued throughout the rest of prehistoric Britain into the medieval period (moats and defended manor houses, for example).

A good example of this is the settlement at Staple Howe (**100**), a small farmstead in the latter part of the sixth century BC; the site occupied a natural knoll and was enclosed by a palisade. Initially the site contained an oval hut which was later replaced by two round huts. The pottery has close affinities with Holland, Belgium and France and the excavator suggested that the inhabitants embarked from the mouth of the Rhine and settled at Staple Howe. This is a superb concept that we have the initial settlement of the first settlers, but the evidence does not support it. The pottery, although imported, has been found on earlier sites elsewhere in Yorkshire. They ate ox, goat, sheep, pig, red and roe deer, fish and wheat. The site catchment included three areas — the high chalk of the Wolds, the long, wide, 'low', wet valley of the vale of Pickering, and the vale of York to the south and west, all of which would have been rich in natural resources.

Brochs, duns and crannogs

As we move further north the sites in Scotland have been referred to in the Bronze Age but the first millennium BC in Scotland can be characterised by

IMPRESSION OF STAPLE HOWE IN THE LAST STAGE OF OCCUPATION

100 *Staple Howe, North Yorkshire. Situated on the northern edge of the Yorkshire Wolds, overlooking the Vale of Pickering. First excavated in May 1951 having been discovered by chance when four people were picnicking on the site. The small knoll was encircled by a timber palisade, with two round houses and a granary inside*

crannogs, brochs and duns. Brochs are the most visually striking and relatively common. The aerial photograph of the broch of Gurness (**colour plate 22**) shows the broch itself, the remains of the tower which might have been 12m (37ft) high. Figure **101** (Dun Telve) shows the internal construction of the broch, with a staircase to the upper floors. Brochs were probably roofed, and each floor level properly spanned. They would have been dark inside but they had lamps. The broch was encircled by three lines of ditch and rampart with an entrance to the east. The broch (which was one aspect of the Iron Age 'settlement') is surrounded by stone-built houses which date from a later period, but which may have been built on earlier houses. Once again the siting of the broch on the edge of a low cliff overlooking the sea emphasises the importance of the sea to the prehistoric communities. The study of the location of brochs and the subject of 'broch-ology' is undergoing a revival but the work of Sir Lindsay Scott in the 1940s showed that the brochs were situated to command an area of farmland which was moderately large by modern farm standards but small given the quality of soil.

Brochs and duns in Scotland have been characterised by topographical location and architectural style, and not in terms of how they function as settlement systems within the economic strategies of the Iron Age. New evidence is coming to light from recent excavations that the people who lived in the brochs all used similar material cultural items but that their diet was less consistent. This latter diversity has led to the suggestion that the inhabitants of the brochs were of a higher status than other Iron Age communities.

One item which has been looked at is the wall width in proportion to height; the thicker the wall the higher the broch. To achieve the same floor area (thin low building, or high thick building) thicker walls would be needed. More floors would have allowed for greater flexibility of use; animal stalling, storage, and living areas.

Duns are related to brochs in that they are stone-built and are often in similar locations. If you look at any OS map of Scotland, you will see the coastal cliff edges and hilltops littered with the gothic writing *dun*. Even those with the same shape and size have different functions because of location. Those near good land will have functioned differently from those on exposed cliff-edges.

The view that brochs and duns can be seen as regional variants in Atlantic culture stone-building tradition (and not a chronological sequence) is expressed well at the sites of Dun Troddan, Dun Telve (brochs) and Dun

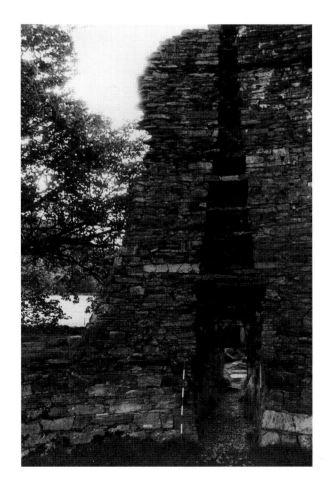

101 *Internal structure of Dun Telve broch.* Copyright: Professor D.W. Harding

Grugaig (dun or semi-broch) in Glen Beag (in north-west Scotland on the way to Skye). Their location is determined by the proximity of good agricultural land. The same point is noted by Mercer about brochs in Hallidale (Caithness) and by Stevenson about duns in Tiree. Ian Morrison in his book on crannogs has also noted that in Loch Awe crannogs do not occur opposite the land which is good for grazing and has a dun situated near it.

Crannogs (**102**) are an important part of the prehistoric settlement pattern. They are not only ubiquitous but they also contain waterlogged organic material, which when excavated reveals much more about the prehistoric way of life than the material from dry-land sites. The drawback with crannogs is their inaccessibility. They are usually situated in the middle of a lake, loch or expanse of water.

The term crannog comes from a Gaelic word *crannag*, or in Irish *crannog*; and the *crann-* element in the word implies 'wood'. As with so many terms they have been accepted as common usage even though a crannog may also refer to uninhabited or totally unaltered islands in lochs and loughs. There has been an increase in the work done on them but there is much more that could

102 *Reconstruction of a crannog from a number of surveys and excavation.* Drawn by Jean Williamson

be studied. Brochs, duns and crannogs should not be studied as isolated monument classes but as part of an integrated landscape pattern so that more information is obtained about their date, function and distribution.

Glastonbury Lake Village

Research on crannogs in England and Wales has not been as fruitful as in Scotland and there is scope for work in the Lake District and the lakes in Wales. There is one site which, although on dry (drained) land now, might have been similar to crannogs 2,000 years ago. The Glastonbury Lake Village is one of the most studied and re-examined of all the Iron Age sites in England (**103** and **colour plate 22**), and one with good preservation.

Over 100 years have elapsed since the discoveries and excavations by Arthur Bulleid began at Glastonbury Lake Village in 1892. In the introduction to the excavation report (published in 1911), Munro said 'In the course of a couple of years the fame of the Glastonbury Lake Village became so great that people flocked from all parts of the country to the site of this singular dwelling place.' It is interesting to note that between 1892 and 1907 a total of £92 18s 6d was collected for 'Entrance fees to the Field'; if we knew how much each person had been charged we could work out the number of paying visitors. It is likely to have been less than sixpence each; if it was threepence each approximately 7,434 people would have visited. In the days before cars, tarmac roads and the great 'heritage industry' this is a considerable number of people, even if it is wrong by a factor of two!

The site was discovered by Arthur Bulleid and has 90 or more low mounds and the whole area was excavated; the site plan (**103**) reveals the complexity of the mounds. The complexity of the site has warranted a number of interpretations and analyses.

David Clarke, an exponent of archaeological theory, proposed a model for each 'unit' of occupation; this model has had its critics (because of its lack of reality) but it is possible to argue that the very existence of the model helped the recent re-interpretations emerge in the way that they did.

Clarke's model attempts to say that there is a modular unit (like a portacabin approach to Iron Age villages) which comprised two sorts of houses in which the major houses and their satellites and the minor house and its ancillaries are divided between 'a major familial, multi-role and activity area on the one hand and a minor, largely female and domestic area'.

Clarke defines seven structural types (I-VII) which are repeatedly reproduced on the site; he interprets this as 'a particular transformation of an otherwise standardized set of relationships between the structural category and every other category'. If I understand this correctly, the suggestion is that throughout the 90 or so mounds at Glastonbury a repeated, standard 'household type' would be found; moreover this building block is also reflected in the total plan for the whole site. The model is thus a reflection of each

103 *Glastonbury Lake Village. Plan of the mounds and palisade (dotted line) and the extent of the excavated area.* After Bulleid, Coles and Coles

household area and the whole site. This may be an interesting theory and provoke some discussion but is it any where near the truth?

The latest re-interpretation has been by John Coles whose work in the Somerset Levels has shown the close relationship prehistoric peoples had with wet, boggy bits of land which modern (post-sixteenth-century) land-use activities drain at an alarming rate. Having worked for so long in the Somerset Levels, John Coles has turned his attention to a re-interpretation of the Glastonbury Lake Village. Apart from completely reworking the theoretical model his scheme also provides a chronological framework for the site. There are four phases for the occupation at Glastonbury. The Early phase which comprised a few hut circles and several sheds, dated around 150 BC; in this phase the platform building began. In the Middle phase the settlement expanded, with new houses being built, a couple of which burnt down, and the palisade around the crannog was started. There was further expansion in the Late phase, with a number of new structures and the completion of the palisade. In the Final contraction phase there were only a few houses occupied, and the site was finally abandoned in AD 50.

This sequence would have seen several families living at the Glastonbury Lake Village in 150 BC, perhaps 70 people in all; this would have expanded to 200 people in the peak (Late phase) with a reduction in numbers in the Final phase to about 100 people. There is the possibility that one or two houses were for the ruling elite, perhaps reserved for the chieftain and his (or her) family.

There would have been satellite farms and settlements which may well have made up a Glastonbury hamlet, but these have not been discovered. There is another Lake village at Meare (6km, 3.75 miles, west of Glastonbury), also excavated by Bulleid and Gray once they had finished work at Glastonbury. Here there are two groups of mounds which were the remains of a late Iron Age village. It has been argued that this site was a summer meeting place for all Iron Age communities around, and unlike Glastonbury Lake Village was seasonally occupied.

The communities at Glastonbury had a well-balanced food supply which consisted of peas, barley, wheat, spelt, pig, and fish. The discovery of small sickles suggest that the crop was cut below the ear leaving the stalks for pasture; grazing for the sheep was necessary as the wool was probably used for more than local needs. The flocks of sheep would perhaps have been wintered in the highlands with summer grazing in the lower, wetter areas. The faunal assemblage also reveals the presence of all types of birds; the list is quite exhaustive in the excavation report – cormorant, heron, bittern, puffin, swan, pelican, teal, golden eye, pintail, shoveller, wigeon, tufted duck, scaup, pochard, red-breasted merganser, coot, crane, little grebe, sea eagle, goshawk, kite, barn owl and carrion crow. The local environment near to the settlement was marsh and mere. Many of birds would have been killed by clay pellets from a sling; some of the birds were very young (pelican, swan and crane) and the evidence is that they were breeding locally. Fish, too, will have formed an important component of the diet, probably roach, trout, shad and perch.

There is also good evidence for metalworking, spinning, pottery manufacture, wood working, basket making, weaving and comb manufacture. There were dice for gambling, and cock spurs for cock fighting.

Glastonbury Lake Village will always remain one of the unique sites in British prehistory not least for its preservation and total excavation; its position in the wet peatlands of the Somerset Levels should make the discovery of a site in a similar position in South Yorkshire less of a surprise. Aerial photography by the late Derrick Riley, a pioneer of aerial photography, discovered this site (**104**); recent excavations have shown these two enclosures to be unique in terms of shape but these well-preserved deposits were drying out. The deposits contain material from the Mesolithic through to the Iron Age but the bank and ditches as seen now are of an Iron Age date. The draining and ploughing has stopped, seen and the site conserved; it is included here as a tribute to the work of Derrick Riley who first started recording cropmarks in the Thames Valley in the 1930s and continued working, worldwide, until 1993.

104 *Sutton Common, South Yorkshire. Aerial photograph of two enclosures which excavations have shown contain Neolithic to Iron Age material; they are now threatened by ploughing and drainage.* Courtesy of Derrick Riley

Oppida

It is easier for us to comprehend the way of life of Iron Age sites – be they hillforts, farmsteads, enclosed sites, open farms or even villages – as they are not too distant from our own experience. There were, however, developments at the end of the Iron Age and at the beginning of the Roman period that are more akin to early town development and should be even more familiar.

Often the classical authors referred to some of the settlements in Britain as *oppida* (Caesar referred to the defended sites in Gaul as *oppida*). Suetonius in his *Life of Vespasian* mentions that Vespasian captured the Isle of Wight and 20 *oppida*; surely this means some of the hillforts of southern England.

Strictly speaking *oppidum* means 'town', but Maiden Castle or Dyke Hills (**colour plate 27**) would have been seen as a town to a visiting Roman. There is, however, a class of site in European archaeology called *oppida*, which usually refers to large urban sites where size and organisation and not defence are the basic defining criteria. In Britain the usage is less clear and strictly the main *oppida* would have been Colchester and St Albans where the large size, low-ground siting and linear dykes (sort of town walls) set them apart from defended hillforts.

John Collis who has written a book on *oppida* favours a definition which has defence as an element in the definition but this must be combined with the internal use, i.e. a town worth defending. Although in European terms *oppida* are important, in the development of towns there are probably only a few examples in southern England which meet the criteria. Roman towns developed partly as a result of the existing Iron Age system but were more influenced by the Roman military geography of Britannia (**105**).

Other landscapes

In moving through the prehistoric settlements by period (Mesolithic to the Iron Age) there was little time to explore certain landscapes which are either so diverse that they cannot be fitted neatly into one time band, or they are so specific and self-contained, yet undated, that they do not easily fall into any scheme. This chapter briefly covers the extremes, using three examples. The first is the Thames Valley, the second a small island off the west coast of Wales, Skomer Island, and the third the area of West Heslerton, in the Vale of Pickering in North Yorkshire.

The Thames Valley

From Gloucestershire in the west to London (**106**) in the east, the Thames Valley contains archaeological deposits of all periods from the Palaeolithic to the Industrial Revolution. Recently it has been the focus of survey and excavation brought about by changes in agriculture since 1945, the development of aerial photography and the need for gravel for all types of construction projects (houses and roads in particular). The cropmark evidence of all the river gravels in Britain has been known about since the seminal work by the RCHME, *A Matter of Time* was published in 1960. This presented an encouraging picture of the wealth of archaeology in gravel areas and a gloomy forecast for the rate of destruction; further cropmark surveys were undertaken in the 1970s, and 1990s. New sites are discovered each year (**colour plates 2 & 18**) and more areas are excavated as the gravel pits inexorably expand. There is not the space here to summarise

105 *'I expect you have heard about Roman roads'*

106 *Location of sites and excavation by the Oxford Archaeological Unit in the Thames Valley.* Copyright Oxford Archaeological Unit

40 years' work but for prehistoric settlement there has been an increase in our knowledge of the area; the gloomy forecast of 1960 has been proved correct in that many archaeological sites have been destroyed, and the number excavated represents a small percentage of what has been destroyed.

The Thames Valley itself has been overworked in comparison to the study of land-use and settlement on the valley slopes. A biased picture is emerging which has little to do with what actually went on in the past; it has more to do with how we have 'accidentally' come to study the past. This is partly determined by our own land-use in which arable cultivation has led to discoveries of cropmarks in river gravels. These sites are also threatened because of our own need for gravel.

Cropmarks reveal important sites but in river valleys there can be a negative correlation between the clarity of the cropmark and preservation; thinner soils produce clearer marks because the buried features are nearer the surface and have been plough-damaged. Cropmarks beneath alluvium are often faint, but are likely to be better preserved.

On the evidence which is emerging from river gravels the population density in the Roman period is argued to have been equal to that of the Middle Ages. The explosion of the population began in the late Iron Age with the intensification of agriculture. In the Bronze Age the settlement pattern in the middle Thames Valley was based on the need for herding livestock although there was some arable activity. Paddocks and wells are absent from early Iron Age sites which suggests arable was the predominant from of agriculture and not cattle. In the middle Iron Age these features come back suggesting a more mixed farming approach, including horse rearing.

George Lambrick has identified three types of site:

1) 'Banjo' enclosures, Mingies Ditch and Watkins Farm (**107**), ditched and hedged farms with funnel-shaped entrances and areas for coralling livestock with pens and paddocks.

2) Open settlements such as Claydon Pike, Port Meadow, and perhaps Gill Mill (**107, 108**), with paddocks – on dry ground within the alluvial floodplain. These were in use for a long time as there were at least two phases were of layout.

3) Small one-phase farmsteads, revealed beneath the alluvial deposits, seasonal and short-lived which specialized pastoralism in the middle Iron Age. The Farmoor settlement is a good example. There would have been summer grazing on the floodplain and the location of settlement dictated by land use. In the Stanton Harcourt area it is now possible to suggest that a series of mixed farms on the second terrace may have formed part of a single community with a variety of pastoral farmsteads on the lower ground, the whole complex occupying the equivalent of about two modern parishes.

In the late Iron Age, at Barton Court Farm, there is evidence of the intensification of arable, the growing of bread wheats, but also horticulture with deeper ploughing on heavier soils and better drainage. This will have assisted the onset of alluviation if poorer valley slopes soils were being ploughed. There appears to have been an increase in enclosure for fields and probably quite large fields; manuring was taking place given scatters of pottery found during fieldwalking. From the research by the Oxford Unit George Lambrick concludes that the importance of pastoralism is under-played in the Iron Age even though arable production expanded, the productivity did not increase (**108**); it was not until the arrival of the Romans that advances in technology and the introduction of new species had a real effect. In the late Iron Age: and early Roman the farms remained much the same in an unchanged landscape structure; the conquest of the Romans was invisible in the Thames Valley. This indicates an agricultural, social and economic system which was working well, was prosperous and not in any need of change. It also assumes a population which was willing to serve a new master, or was it that the master (the Romans) paid the right price?

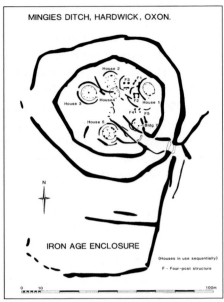

107 *Excavation plan of the Iron Age enclosures at Watkins Farm and Mingies Ditches.*
Copyright Oxford Archaeological Unit

The Thames Valley has been the subject of a huge amount of work over the last 40 years, with surveys and excavations, and it is interesting to contrast the results for the Iron Age of the re-mapping of all the cropmark evidence from aerial photographs (as part of NMP). In the Bronze Age the predominant features were round barrows but for the Iron Age there were 184 'enclosures', 162 hut circles and six hillforts recorded. This reinforces the biases in the evidence between the two periods.

So often archaeologists are expected to provide the answer now; this can be achieved for a few specific questions. For the central, fundamental questions about sites or regions archaeological research takes a long time and it will be many years before we fully understand the archaeology of the Thames Valley. Fortunately, the agents of destruction in the area (gravel extraction especially) are now being levied and the funds raised by this levy are being used to improve our understanding and enjoyment of the Thames Valley.

Skomer Island

In complete contrast to the length and complexity of the Thames Valley is the small island off the coast of west Wales, Skomer Island. It is well known for its wildlife, especially birdlife (the largest colony of Manx shearwaters in the world). The island was first archaeologically recorded by Professor Grimes in the 1950s. More recently, under the supervision of Dr John Evans of Cardiff University, the island's archaeology has been mapped and recorded by students;

aerial photographs helped in locating and identifying sites (**109**). The system of field walls and settlements is clearly visible and a visit to the island is worthwhile; time your visit so that the archaeology will be visible (the bracken obscures the archaeology from June onwards) – but beware of the birds!

In the reports on the field survey it is clear that something is known about the settlements, and the field pattern, even damming water. There is the suggestion that two of the features are 'saunas'; there is growing amount of evidence that 'sweat boxes' were used in prehistory from a number of sites. This removes us further from the filthy savage idea of our ancestors. The major problem with the Skomer landscape is that we know so little about it in terms of who lived there (an estimate has been between 100 and 200 people at any one time), and why was it abandoned? What was the date and length of occupation? John Evans in his short guide (*Prehistoric Farmers of Skomer Island*) argues that the occupation was short-lived, as there is little evidence of the fields being sub-divided or extended. We do not know its date, but it is typical of later prehistoric settlements in the west of Britain; what made Skomer unique is the survival of the almost complete system of a prehistoric farming community.

To experience what life must have been like in prehistory is impossible but by visiting places like Skomer, the western Isles of Scotland and Orkney (to

108 *The area near Stanton Harcourt in the Thames Valley showing the relationship of prehistoric sites with each other and the different geologies..* Copyright: Oxford Archaeological Unit

KEY

OXFORD AND KIMMERIDGE CLAY

CORALLIAN SAND

ALLUVIUM

GRAVEL TERRACES

LATE NEO-BA MONUMENTS

EARLY-MID IA SETTLEMENTS

LIA-EARLY RB SETTLEMENTS

LATER RB SETTLEMENTS

RB TRACKWAYS

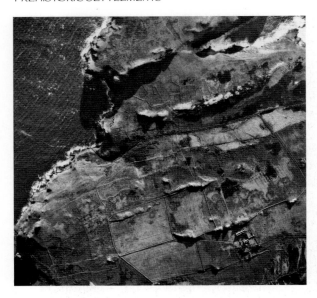

109 *Aerial photograph of part of Skomer Island.* Cambridge University Collection of Air Photographs: copyright reserved

name just a few) it is possible to experience a flavour of the environment in which they lived. The high bird population, especially migratory species, must have been an important food resource; if the bird populations are high now what must they have been like 3,000 years ago?

West Heslerton

Intensive investigations using surveys and excavations over the past 25 years in the landscape around West Heslerton, have produced dramatic discoveries of sites from the Neolithic to the Anglian. The innovative approaches by Dominic Powlesland and his team were developed as traditional methods of survey could not penetrate the layers of wind-blown sand which had buried the sites. Situated at the foot of the chalk scarp, which defines the southern edge of the Vale of Pickering, the wind-blown sand proved fertile agricultural land and the effects of deep ploughing have been damaging the sites. Excavations, although on a large scale, have only covered a small percentage of what remains beneath the surface as figure **110** vividly shows. There are many Iron Age (and earlier) sites represented here and this type of information is crucial for improving our understanding of Britain's rich archaeological resources, but also for planning its future preservation, management and enjoyment for future generations.

During this journey through prehistoric Britain one theme has been ever present – that new discoveries are constantly changing and making us re-assess our interpretations. The number and distribution of one type of site, burnt mounds, has expanded dramatically in the past decade. As with so many new discoveries, once one or two have been found many more are found once people have their eye in for these fairly non-descript features. The mounds are

110 *Geophysical survey image showing a segment of the West Heslerton landscape between the foot of the Yorkshire Wolds and the wetlands which once existed in the centre of the Vale of Pickering.* Landscape research centre

indicators of settlements in that the stones they contain have been split by being heated. They represent places where stones have been heated and dropped into water either for cooking (stews for a feast) or for the saunas or sweat houses referred to on Skomer Island. By contrast there are many sites which have been recorded for some years, but their significance has yet to be realised. It has always been a surprise to me how few prehistoric settlements have been discovered in the Lake District, but there are some well-preserved ones on the margins of lakes and at the foot of some impressive mountains (**colour plate 26**).

Too often professional archaeologists are expected to know the answers to all the questions, but usually there are more questions than solutions and although there are large amounts of information for us all to make interpretations there are many more sites which require research and investigation than there are archaeologists.

7

CONCLUSIONS

New initiatives and survey methods

As has already been mentioned there is more archaeological activity in the country than ever before, yet archaeology is still not a fundamental part of teaching in schools. Prehistory warrants special mention in a recent parliamentary report (published in February 2003) by stating that 'Prehistory should be part of all national curricula.'

The increase in archaeological investigations is benefiting from a combination of old and new techniques. Not only are there new remote sensing devices – especially machines with laser beams (Lidar) which have already been mentioned – but there are also multi-spectral imaging sensors, which are being assessed for their archaeological potential. These are not just new toys but are capable of helping us understand the fundamental question 'how reliable is the information we have?' Throughout this book I have stressed the fragility of the evidence on which we base our assumptions and as archaeology becomes a more important part of our everyday lives, especially through the media of television and the internet, a greater understanding of the nature of the evidence is required. This is equally true for those involved in the management and presentation of the country's archaeology. So often we are able to protect sites which we can see, either from the air or one the ground; however buried archaeological sites require protection too, because they have greater potential for providing more reliable information in the future, as their material may have been preserved in waterlogged conditions and they will not have suffered erosion from ploughing and desiccation from drainage.

There are two initiatives which are attempting to tackle our lack of information and understanding. The first has already been referred to, English Heritage's National Mapping Programme (NMP), and the other is a national project of Historic Landscape Characterization (HLC). The NMP aims to increase our understanding of the historic environment through interpretation of aerial photographs and produce a map, with an accompanying archaeological record of all the sites examined. So far some 30 per cent of England has been mapped, with very interesting results from all periods but in certain areas our understanding of prehistory has been enhanced considerably. In Cornwall there has been a dramatic increase in the number of *rounds*, prehistoric settlements, and in the area around the Camel Estuary, prehistoric land use becomes abundantly clear when the settlement sites are situated on the anciently enclosed land (which is low-lying and fertile), whereas the burials are all on the recently enclosed land, the higher heath and moorland. These distinctions of enclosing land have been developed as part of the Historic Landscape Characterization project which aims to characterize the historic potential of all parts of England, so that we improve our understanding of the potential for the discovery of sites. Thus the absence of evidence is not used as evidence of absence.

Archaeology is a combination of obtaining information, interpreting, analysing, and then modelling new and old evidence; as a subject, it is always changing. A major theme of prehistoric archaeology is the changes which take place over thousands of years. The landscape is ever-changing either as a result of human interference or because of the global changes which have taken place in the last 8,000 years. Similarly human adaptation to a whole range of factors (social, ritual, environmental, and ecological) changes through time. This results in a kaleidoscopic picture and makes the study of prehistoric settlements both frustrating and challenging. It is the reason that there are no absolute answers to the questions about social organisation and settlement pattern.

The theme of interpretation and re-interpretation is also part of the kaleidoscope and inevitably our knowledge of prehistoric settlements will increase, and interpretations will develop. To allow this to happen we have to be aware of the different scales at which prehistoric people and twenty-first-century society operate. Often the scale can be defined in distances, or in expectations. The example of Dartmoor as a central place in prehistory but considered marginal today is a good example.

The fact that we discuss long distance trade in the Neolithic reflects that prehistoric people travelled very long distances. We travel long distances today but we expect to travel hundreds of miles in a day, whereas travelling the same distance might have been a seasonal activity or on a yearly or five-yearly cycle in prehistory.

Similarly, if we consider the daily experience of living in a prehistoric settlement and their 'world', the scale is significant. For hunters, gatherers or farmers an intricate knowledge of the very local area would have been a prerequisite for the survival of the community. The challenge which faces archaeology is the way in which we study the inter-relationship of sites in any area. We need to know the contemporaneity of sites, the hierarchy of sites, and we need to examine the function of sites. So often we have only the midden, the rubbish dump, on which to build our theories. These are important biases to our understanding of prehistoric communities; it is difficult to understand any human community if we only rely on what they left behind.

Additionally, our techniques of recovery are biased. Aerial photography is one aspect which has helped the study of prehistoric settlements, but it is not without its limitations. Recent work in the Thames Valley has shown that there are large areas of cropmarks, but that the other supposed blank areas contain as much, if not more information when excavated. I have made liberal use of aerial photographs to illustrate the sites mentioned in this book, but their major use is in providing information for maps which contain archaeological information. At the appropriate scale the maps will be useful in studying the distribution of sites, but they can also help to preserve sites, by providing the information in a usable form to the appropriate body. Modern archaeology is as much about understanding the past as it is about preserving the fragile remains, and aerial photography has been a significant factor in these two aspects.

Chris Taylor argued in 1972 that the present rate of destruction of archaeological sites was so fast that by AD 2000 there would be nothing left for archaeologists to do. In 1972 the end of the millennium must have seemed an eternity away; now it is already history. Surveys, on the ground and in the air, are going on continuously in Britain, in particular the National Mapping Programme funded by English Heritage, but many others funded by other government departments, Cadw, Historic Scotland, the Royal Commissions, Archaeological Units and Trusts and county archaeologists.

The vast increase in information has stimulated more synthesising and consideration of 'what does it all mean?' In the role of the great synthesiser, famous from Kent Flannery's *Early MesoAmerican Village*, it is apposite to use the recent work of Richard Bradley. He suggests three phases of interpretation for prehistory in terms of linking or understanding ritual and everyday activities: the first is in the tradition of creating monuments that recalled an ancient past (real or imagined); the second reflects those monuments whose origins are to be found in the natural topography of Britain; and the third is the symbolic elaboration of the house. These are not chronologically dependent and are useful concepts to use when assessing any site or landscape.

The study of archaeology is the study of change, which is sometimes referred to as progress. Technologically there may have been progress in the development of sophisticated computers and machinery, but socially has anything changed in the last 8,000 years? As a species we are still learning to live together (or not live together) in towns and cities, or in isolated communities. Throughout prehistory and history there has been conflict between human communities and this aspect of human behaviour is represented in the archaeological record for prehistoric settlements.

The extent to which we interpret, or emphasise, any particular aspect of prehistory will be a function of our own background and beliefs.

SITES TO VISIT

A short list of archaeological guides is listed under Further reading. If you have no restraints on your time and a complete set of Ordnance Survey 1:50,000 Landranger maps for the whole country, you can happily spend years visiting every site marked as an antiquity. Many of these sites are settlements or field systems; even if they are burial mounds, henges or stone circles, at least you will be visiting places of prehistoric interest. The OS map *Ancient Britain*, also provides a very good introduction to prehistoric sites in Britain.

Many of the sites are on private land and permission must be obtained prior to any visit. Public footpaths often run near or through many of the sites and these paths are marked on the Landranger maps.

Northern England

Carrock Fell: The most dramatic setting for a stone-built hillfort in northern Cumbria; when visiting, consider its potential as a Neolithic site and not just an Iron Age hillfort. The steep climb up from east is well worth the effort. 6km (3.75) SSE of Caldbeck.

Castle Crag: An imposing setting for a small fort with two rock-cut ditches overlooking Mardale (now Hawsewater Reservoir) in Cumbria.

Crosby Ravensworth: A series of settlements surviving as earthworks to the south, south-east and west of the village of Crosby Ravensworth, Cumbria dating to the prehistoric and Roman periods. Survey plans were published in the *Inventory for Westmorland*, RCHME (1936) 78-92.

Eston Nab: This hillfort overlooks the industrial heart of Middlesbrough but is a reminder of the changes which have taken place in the last 3,000 years. It is located south-east of Middlesbrough, south of the A174.

Great Urswick, Cumbria: An Iron Age hillfort on a limestone plateau with perhaps earlier remains. 4km (2.5 miles) SSE of Ulverston.

Ingleborough: One of the highest hillforts in England. Remains of hut circles with stone foundations and a stone rampart. Possibly one of the strongholds of the Brigantes tribe, situated on the top of a plateau in the centre of the Pennines.

Hartsop Hall Settlement. Two miles east of the Brothers Water Hotel, Patterdale, off the Kirkstone Pass Road. This site is in a very impressive location but is on private land (**colour plate 26**).

Ingram valley, Northumberland: An area of well-preserved settlements and field systems on either side of the Beamish river. Most are on private land, but those which are accessible via a public footpath are marked on the Landranger Map no. 81. 16km (10 miles) NNW of Rothbury.

Mam Tor, Derbyshire: The impressive position and ramparts of this hillfort make it a favourite location for walkers and hang gliders. Inside the ramparts are numerous platforms presumably for huts and houses; there is evidence of earlier Bronze Age material on the site.

Yeavering, Northumberland: Stone-built hillfort with hut circles, a round cairn and extramural terraces. Very commanding position on the top of a steeply rising fell, Yeavering Bell. The hillfort overlooks the Millfield Basin, an area rich in prehistoric archaeology and two Anglo-Saxon royal palaces.

Yorkshire Dales: Numerous settlements and field systems especially around Grassington, but elsewhere throughout the Yorkshire Dales National Park. Further information can be obtained from the local National Park Offices in Grassington and from the Landranger maps (98 & 99).

Southern England

Bodbury Ring, Shropshire: A small triangular hillfort with very steep approaches and commanding a strategic position in these border lands. Access is via the Church Stretton golf course.

Butser Ancient Farm: A reconstruction of an Iron Age farm, with large and small round houses, industrial working areas, fields with crops, sheep and cattle. Near Chalton, Hampshire (**colour plate 14**). www.butser.org.uk.

Carn Brea, Cornwall: The largest Iron Age hillfort in Cornwall of 18ha (46 acres) with hut circles inside. The eastern summit has revealed evidence of Neolithic occupation.

Carn Euny, Cornwall: Iron Age to Romano-British hamlet, with three interlocking courtyard houses and other round houses. Within the settlement is a well-preserved fogou.

Castle an Dinas, Cornwall: A well-preserved Iron Age hillfort with three ramparts and an earlier Bronze Age cairn.

Chysauster, Cornwall: The best preserved example of a courtyard house hamlet, only 1 mile east of Castle an Dinas hillfort. The visible remains are Romano-British but there is good evidence for the earlier settlement (**colour plate 25**).

Crickley Hill, Gloucestershire: Originally a Neolithic causewayed camp but developing into an Iron Age promontory fort dating from the sixth century BC. Now part of a Country Park it is a good place for day out or picnic. Stunning views overlooking the Vale of Gloucester.

Danebury, Hampshire: This is one of the few Iron Age hillforts to have been extensively excavated. In the Bronze Age the summit was marked by a number of ritual pits. The first Iron Age hillfort was constructed in the fifth century BC and it underwent four major redevelopments before finally being abandoned some time after the Romans' arrival (**80**).

Dartmoor, Devon: The Dartmoor landscape, especially the reave system, has to be experienced and this can be achieved by walking through its moors and valleys. Individual sites can be selected by looking at the Landranger maps, but Grimspound and the Rider's Rings (see below) are two accessible sites (**41**).

Flag Fen Visitor Centre, near Peterborough, Cambridgeshire: Based on excavations of Bronze Age wooden structures and reconstructions of a Bronze Age Lake Village and round houses. Educational guided tours are available. Open every day from 10am to 5pm. For further information ring 01733 313414 or see www.flagfen.com (**colour plate 10**).

Grimspound, Devon: A stone-built Bronze Age settlement on the east side of Dartmoor. Within the stone walls are a numerous hut circles and cattle pens.

Hambledon Hill, Dorset: This long ridge contains the remains of a Neolithic causewayed camp and an enormous Iron Age hillfort. Research and excavation have shown that the causewayed camp was abandoned after being attacked. The hillfort developed and expanded to its present size during the Iron Age (cf. Maiden Castle) (**29**).

Hod Hill, Dorset: One of the largest hillforts to be taken by Vespasian in AD 43. The Iron Age hillfort contains a Roman fort in its north-western corner. (Visit Hambledon Hill at the same time. **68, 72**).

Maiden Castle, Dorset: Comparable to Hambledon Hill in that a Neolithic causewayed camp is contained within a multi-vallate hillfort. Excavations have taken place twice during this century and the hillfort developed to be one of the largest and most important in southern England during the Iron Age (**7**).

Rider's Rings, Devon: A Bronze Age stone-built settlement comprising two enclosures or pounds which contain numerous huts and possible stock pens (**42**).

Rough Tor, Cornwall: On this summit there are a number of oval enclosures with hut circles which are the remains of Bronze Age and Iron Age settlements, possibly hillforts (**colour plate 5**).

Stowe's Pound, Cornwall: The two stone enclosures on Stowe's Hill are of different sizes and are perhaps Neolithic origins with occupation continuing into the Bronze Age. The larger encircles the summit and contains over 100 house platforms, the smaller oval enclosure is attached to the southern end of the larger hillfort (**colour plate 9**).

The Trundle, Sussex: Neolithic causewayed camp and an octagonal Iron Age hillfort commanding views in all directions.

Windmill Hill, Wiltshire: One of the first causewayed camps to be identified in the 1930s. With good access and numerous round barrows within the three encircling ditches, it is one of the classic sites in Wessex. Near Avebury and Silbury Hill (**26**).

Wales

Burfa Camp: An impressive multi-vallate hillfort set within too many trees, but recent clearance has revealed the entrance more clearly.

Caerau Hillfort: Near Ely, Cardiff in the east end of the Vale of Glamorgan. Three ramparts surround a natural plateau to provide the setting of one of the strongest forts in South Wales.

Carn Goch: a hillfort with a stone rampart enclosing 10ha (24 acres) in a very commanding position, 5km (3 miles) north-east of Llandeilo.

Castel Henllyss, Iron Age Hillfort. Pembrokeshire, Wales. The hillfort dates to 600 BC. There are ongoing excavations and experimental archaeology, including reconstructed thatched Iron Age roundhouses. Open April to November 10am to 5pm. 01239 891319. www.castellhenllys.com.

Tre'r Ceiri: Known as the 'town of the giants' this stone-built hillfort encloses the summit of one of three hills overlooking the Lleyn peninsula and the coast. Within the ramparts are numerous stone huts. In the Roman period an outer rampart was added, more huts were built and the earlier huts re-modelled (**73**).

Scotland

Broch of Gurness, Orkney: This broch is one of the most impressive in Britain. The tower would have originally stood 12m (37ft) high. The stone-built settlement surrounding the tower will have had Iron Age origins but as visible today represent first millennium AD houses (**colour plate 22**).

Dun Carloway, Lewis: One of the best preserved brochs in Scotland, containing typical broch features such as two side cells leading off the courtyard.

Dun Telve, Lochalsh: With only part of the wall of this broch standing it is possible to see the internal broch structure. There are a number of stone outbuildings which may have been stock pens (**89**).

Finavon, Angus: A good example of vitrified (stones fused by heat) fort. The ramparts are over 6m (20ft) thick and were probably timber laced.

Jarslhof, Shetland: Occupation at this stone-built settlement site began in the Bronze Age and continued until the seventeenth century AD. The prehistoric settlement consists of round and oval houses and workshops.

Mousa Broch, Shetland: With the tower standing 13m (46ft) this broch is the best preserved in Britain; at its base the tower is 15m (50ft) in diameter.

The Scottish Crannog Centre: A reconstructed crannog, built on wooden piles, on the shores of Loch Tay, 8 miles west of Aberfeldy, open daily March and November.

Skara Brae, Orkney: Neolithic village with interconnecting stone-built houses. One of the most famous sites of British prehistory and situated on the coast it is well worth a visit (**31**).

Woden Law, Roxburghshire: A strategic setting for a hillfort which continued its influence into the Roman period as it commanded the area close to Dere Street, the Roman road from York to the Firth of Forth (**55**).

FURTHER READING

Archaeological guides

Darvill, Tim, Paul Stamper & Jane Timby, 2002. *England: an Oxford archaeological guide to sites from earliest times to AD 1600*, Oxford.

Darvill, T.C., 1996. *Prehistoric Britain from the Air*, Cambridge University Press, Cambridge.

Dyer, James, 1973. *Southern England: An Archaeological Guide*, Faber.

Houlder, Christopher, 1978. *Wales: An Archaeological Guide*, Faber.

MacSween, Ann, & Mick Sharp, 1989. *Prehistoric Scotland*, Batsford, London.

Cornwall Archaeological Unit, 1990. *Cornwall's Archaeological Heritage*, Twelveheads, Truro.

Cornwall Archaeological Unit, 1992. *Scilly's Archaeological Heritage*, Twelveheads, Truro.

Ritchie, Anna, & Graham Ritchie, 1990. *The Ancient Monuments of Orkney*, Historic Scotland, HMSO, Edinburgh.

General reading

Audouze, Françoise, & Olivier Büchenschütz, 1989. *Towns, Villages and Countryside of Celtic Europe*, Batsford, London.

Bender B., Sue Hamilton & Chris Tilley, 1997. Leskernick: Stone Worlds; Alternative Narratives; Nested Landscapes. *Proceedings of the Prehistoric Society* 63, p.147–178.

Bewley, R.H., 2001. Understanding England's Historic Landscapes: An aerial perspective. *Landscapes* Vol. 2 No. 1, p.74–84

Bowden, Mark, (ed.), 1999. *Unravelling the Landscape. An Inquisitive Approach to Archaeology*, Tempus, Stroud.

Bradley, Richard, 1978. *The Prehistoric Settlement of Britain*, Routledge, Kegan & Paul.

Bradley, Richard, 1993. Altering the Earth. *The 1992 Rhind lectures*. Society of Antiquaries of Scotland Monograph Series Number 8, Edinburgh.

Brück, Joanna, (ed.), 2001. *Bronze Age Landscapes. Tradition and Transformation*, Oxbow, Oxford.

Burgess, Colin, 1980. *The Age of Stonehenge*, Dents, London.

Coles, Bryony, & John Coles, 1986. *Sweet Track to Glastonbury: the Somerset Levels in Prehistory*, Thames & Hudson, London.

Cunliffe, Barry, 1975. *Iron Age Communities in Britain*, Routledge, Kegan & Paul, London (new edition 1993).

Cunliffe B., 2000. *The Danebury Environs Programme. Prehistory of a Wessex Landscape*, English Heritage & Oxford University Committee for Archaeology Monograph 48.

Cunliffe B., & C. Poole, 2000. *The Danebury Environs Programme. Prehistory of a Wessex Landscape*, English Heritage & Oxford University Committee for Archaeology Monographs 49-54.

Darvill, Tim, 1987. *Prehistoric Britain*, Batsford, London.

Dyer, James, 1992. *Hillforts of England and Wales*, Shire Archaeology, Princes Risborough.

Fleming, Andrew, 1988. *The Dartmoor Reaves: Investigating Prehistoric Land Divisions*, Batsford, London.

Fowler, Peter, 1983. *The Farming of Prehistoric Britain*, Cambridge University Press, Cambridge.

Fowler, Peter, 2002. *Farming in the First Millennium AD*. Cambridge University Press, Cambridge.

Green, Miranda, (ed.), 1995. *The Celtic World*, Routledge, London & New York.

Greene, Kevin, 2002. *Archaeology: an introduction*, Routledge, London.

Hogg, A.H.A., 1978. *British Hill-Forts: An Index*, British Archaeological Reports 62, Oxford.

Lubbock, John, 1865. *Pre-historic Times*. Williams and Norgate, London.

Mercer, Roger, 1990. *Causewayed Enclosures*, Shire Archaeology, Princes Risborough.

Mellars, Paul, (ed.), 1978, *The Early Postglacial Settlement of Northern Europe*, Duckworth, London.

Norfolk Museums Service, 1987. *Norfolk from the Air*, Norfolk Museum Service, Norwich.

O'Kelly, Michael, 1989. *Early Ireland*, Cambridge University Press, Cambridge.

Oswald, A., C. Dyer & M. Barber, 2001. *The Creation of Monuments. Neolithic Causewayed Enclosures in the British Isles*, English Heritage, Swindon.

Palmer, R., 1984. *Danebury: An Iron Age Hillfort in Hampshire, An Aerial Photographic Interpretation of its Environs*, RCHME Supplementary Series No. 6.

Pearson, Mike Parker, 1993. *Bronze Age Britain*, Batsford/English Heritage, London.

Piggot, Stuart, 1985. *William Stukeley. An 18th century Antiquary*, Thames and Hudson, London.

Pryor, Francis, 1991. *Flag Fen: Prehistoric Fenland Centre*, Batsford/English Heritage, London.

Pryor, Francis, 1998. *Farmers in Prehistoric Britain*, Tempus, Stroud.

Renfrew, Colin, 1974. *British Prehistory: a new outline*, Duckworth, London.

Renfrew, & Cunliffe, 1997. *Science and Stonehenge*, Oxford University Press, Oxford.

Riley, Derrick, 2000. *Aerial Archaeology in Britain*, Shire Archaeology, Princes Risborough.

Sharples, Niall, 1991. *Maiden Castle*, Batsford/English Heritage, London.

Stoertz, C., 1997. *Ancient Landscapes of the Yorkshire Wolds*, RCHME, Swindon.

Thomas, Julian, 1991. *Re-Thinking the Neolithic*, Cambridge University Press, Cambridge.

Thomas, Julian, 1999. *Understanding the Neolithic*, Routledge, London.

Whittle, Alisdair, 1997. 'Sacred Mound Holy Rings. Silbury Hill and the West Kennet palisade enclosures: a Later Neolithic complex in north Wiltshire'. Oxbow Monograph 74.

Wilson, David, 1982. *Air Photo Interpretation for Archaeologists*, Tempus, Stroud.

Hogg, A.H.A. 1978. *British Hill-Forts: An Index*. British Archaeological Reports 62, Oxford.

Useful addresses

The Prehistoric Society, founded in 1935, is the only national body concerned exclusively with the study of prehistory. It has over 2,000 members and provides its membership with a regular newsletter, *PAST*, an annual *Proceedings of the Prehistoric Society*, Study Tours and Conferences. For more information write to the Prehistoric Society, Institute of Archaeology, University College London,, 31–34 Gordon Square, London WC1H 0PY.

NMR. The National Monuments Record. English Heritage. NMRC, Kemble Drive, Swindon, SN2 2GZ. The national archive which contains archaeological and architectural surveys and records for England.

RCHAMW. The Royal Commission on the Ancient and Historical Monuments of Wales. Crown Buildings, Plas Crug, Aberystwyth. Dyfed. SY23 2HP. The national body of survey and record for Wales.

RCHAMS. The Royal Commission on the Ancient and Historical Monuments of Scotland. John Sinclair House, 16 Bernard Terrace, Edinburgh. EH8 9NX. The national body of survey and record for Scotland.

The Unit for Landscape Modelling, formerly Cambridge University Committee for Aerial Photography (CUCAP). The Mond Building, Free School Lane, Cambridge, CB2 3RF. Tel. 01223 334578 Fax: 01223 334400. Website: aerial@cam.ac.uk. The Collection may be visited by members of the public during normal office hours. Photographs cannot be borrowed but prints can be purchased; orders ordinarily take about a month. Prices depend on print size. Copyright is retained by the University or the Crown.

INDEX

Numbers in **bold** refer to illustrations